RACE, DISCOURSE AND LABOURISM

This book documents the Labour Party's construction of the concept of race in political discourse from the 1930s Indian independence negotiations and the defence of Jews from anti-Semitic attack in East London. The author argues that in these historical processes Labour construed a range of negative significances for black citizenship and multi-culturalism and, despite recasting its approach to race in the 1960s and early 1970s, Labour is still unable to sanction officially the effective representation of black voices in its own ranks. The study shows that Labour has not only tolerated racial inequality, but it has given it important political direction.

Race, Discourse and Labourism is about political processes. It is about the theoretical and political analysis of how race was constructed and sustained as a category in British postwar politics. This study will be of interest to students of politics, race and ethnicity, as well as those who campaign in the Labour Party for racial equality.

Caroline Knowles is a Senior Lecturer at the Polytechnic of East London and Visiting Professor at the Simon Fraser University in British Columbia, Canada. She has been researching, writing and teaching about race since the late 1970s in Britain, West Africa and Canada.

RACE, DISCOURSE AND LABOURISM

Caroline Knowles

London and New York

First published in 1992
by Routledge
11 New Fetter Lane, London EC4P 4EE

Simultaneously published in the USA and Canada
by Routledge
a division of Routledge, Chapman and Hall, Inc.
29 West 35th Street, New York, NY 10001

© 1992 Caroline Knowles

Typeset in Baskerville by
NWL Editorial Services, Langport, Somerset

Printed and bound in Great Britain
by Biddles Ltd, Guildford and King's Lynn

British Library Cataloguing in Publication Data

A catalogue record for this book is available from the British Library.

Library of Congress Cataloging in Publication Data

Knowles, Caroline, 1954–
Race, discourse, and labourism / Caroline Knowles.
p. cm.
Includes bibliographical references and index.
1. Great Britain–Race relations–Government policy.
2. Great Britain–Emigration and immigration–Government policy.
3. Great Britain–Politics and government–1936–
4. Labour Party (Great Britain) I. Title.
DA125.A1K58 1992
323.1'41–dc20   92–4311
CIP

ISBN 0–415–05012–X

To the memory of Jackie

CONTENTS

PREFACE

This work has long been in preparation. It began as a PhD thesis at City University in the mid-1970s, at a time when student activists were regularly drawn into street battles with the National Front, and when the Labour's Party stance on race provided little hope of improvement. Racial conflict, racist immigration procedures and race relations legislation which provided little in the way of redress for racial disadvantage characterise the political landscape of this period. Academic concern with race at this time focused on the notion that the working class itself was racist, and not the vehicle of social transformation that those of us who identified with marxism had hoped. It was this contention which initiated this work which was concerned to investigate the nature of the political agency with which working class representation was most closely associated. Significantly, in the long time it has taken to prepare this volume, many changes have occurred in race politics, and in the nature of labourism. Had this work been completed in the 1970s a very different book would have resulted. However, its essential purpose remains the same, and that is to examine whether the Labour Party may be an effective force for race equality in Britain. The fact that it is possible to write in such a detailed way about the Labour Party is a tribute to its openness to public scrutiny, and the analysis offered in this volume, though critical, is offered in the hope that eventually labour will be able to provide political direction in the mainstream of British politics for building a multi-racial society which sustains, rather than denies, human equality.

During its lengthy preparation this book has involved research in India, it has lived in West Africa, mostly in East London and was finally completed in Canada. Life in these various locations has served its own particular reminders that race is the most significant, dangerous and unacceptable form of social inequality, and that British colonialism still has a great deal to answer for.

Caroline Knowles

ACKNOWLEDGEMENTS

Thanks are due to Stephan Feuchtwang who, in his long association with this work, has provided important criticism and comment. I should also like to thank colleagues in the Race, Culture and Policy Research Unit at the City University, London, and particularly Alrick Cambridge and Kazim Khan. Kingsley Abram, Virendra Sharma, the late Fenner Brockway, Jim Benningfield, W.J. Davies, and Dr Levenberg have all provided important background material through interviews, and for this I thank them. Thanks to Sami Zubaida for comments on earlier versions of this. The staff of numerous libraries and archives have been generous with their time, and I should like to thank particularly the Labour Party archivist Stephen Bird, the Labour Party Librarian, the staff of the British Library and the Official Publications Library, the Marx Memorial Library, the British Newspaper Library, India House Library and Records, Westminster Reference Library, Bethnal Green Library, Hendon Public Library and Archives, the National Museum of Labour History, the Nehru Memorial Library in Delhi, the London School of Economics Library, the Institute of Race Relations Library, Nuffield College Library and the City University Library. Thanks are due to the *Jewish Chronicle*, to Hendon South Labour Party for allowing me to see their records, to Annette Braithwaite for help with research, to the (then) Social Science Research Council for funding, and to colleagues at the LaMarsh Programme at York University, Toronto, for important back-up facilities during the final stages of preparation of the manuscript. Thanks also to John Urry. Thanks to Prue Chamberlayne for discussion and moral support. Thanks to Daniel, James,

Alan and Philippa Weitz for help with the final stages of manuscript preparation. Recognising that books do not get written by female academics with small children unless time and space can be created, I should like to thank Michael Rustin and my colleagues at the Polytechnic of East London for ensuring that I got the time free from teaching that I needed to complete this. Thanks are also due to David Mofford, for lengthy debate as well as support of a more practical kind. Thanks to my family and friends, especially Eric and June Litton, Patrick Knowles and Norma Jones for their support and for making life pleasant. Finally thanks to Jessica and William who tolerate most philosophically my absences and preoccupations.

This volume owes many intellectual debts. It offers an approach to race which has developed out of my teaching in adult education in London, at the University of Miaduguri in Nigeria and at the Polytechnic of East London. Whilst challenges from students and colleagues have not always been comfortable they have undoubtedly helped me develop an analysis of race. I owe an intellectual debt to colleagues in these various institutions, and especially to other members of the Race, Culture and Policy Research Unit at the City University in London. For the views expressed in this volume I, of course, take full responsibility.

INTRODUCTION

Britain is in no sense a multi-racial community. It is a political community fraught with racial tension and racial inequality. Statements about human brotherhood and social cohesion, uttered by the labour movement, cannot obscure the fact that in Britain, a visible minority are socially disadvantaged in ways which impinge upon every facet of their lives. Black Britons suffer the indignity of physical attack, low wages and racist allocations of goods and social facilities. What kind of a community can possibly tolerate these inequalities? Labour and Conservative governments, in turn, have presided over this community in which there is profound division and discord. Both parties are equally to blame for the political conditions which produced this community. Both parties are responsible for pernicious immigration controls, and ineffective race relations legislation. Both are guilty of giving political direction to a society which supports a web of racist practices. But there is a crucial difference between them. Conservatism lacks a conception of social justice which can support a multi-racial community of equal opportunity. Labour does not. Labourism has a conception of social justice which can support these political objectives. Why then has it failed to act upon it? Why has it tolerated racial inequality? Unfortunately labour has done more than tolerate racial inequality, it has given it political direction.

Notions of racial difference lie behind some of the most damaging and significant forms of social inequality in Britain today. Racial distinctions are social categories generated around our society's entire range of social practices and actions.[1] Whenever public housing is distributed, when building societies

1

decide to grant loans, when general practitioners dispense treatment or drugs, the opportunity arises for racial differences to be generated or sustained. Notions of racial difference are constructed by societies, their organisations, institutions, their practices and actions, and the human agents who give them force. They are excavated through the forms of statement and documentation of organisations and institutions: their texts. Political processes are highly significant. They give direction and impetus throughout a society. They provide a focus for debate and disagreement. This book excavates a part of the political landscape in which notions of racial difference provide a focus for unequal treatment. It traces the ways in which conceptions of race were generated by the Labour Party, the ways in which race was raised as a political issue, and the political context in which it was sustained. It asks: What does the Labour Party understand by the term race? Where does that understanding come from? And what is the framework of assumptions in which it is made possible? Notions of racial difference have no ontological existence. Like other concepts race is given a meaning in the contexts in which it is used. It is constructed in the discourses in which it occurs.[2]

Although the Labour Party has a conception of social justice, it has not always applied this to black people. Its conception of social justice has, however, led it to state a commitment to racial equality on which it may be confronted. Despite its exclusion from political power since 1979, labour is still the biggest opposition party. It has demonstrated its capacity for government, and it represents the best chance that racial inequality will become a political concern in mainstream politics. Labour now has a substantial black voice. There are four black MPs for the first time in British postwar history. Many constituency labour parties have unofficial black sections giving political leadership on issues of concern to black populations. Inner city town halls have black mayors and black councillors with experience in dealing with racism locally. Black Britons are demanding action on racial equality. When labour next forms a government it will have to address racism; it has publicly committed itself to so doing. The political conditions of the 1990s are right for labour to have its hand forced over race issues. If the Labour Party fails to deliver, it will lose black support, and the opportunity to recast social democratic politics in Britain in the direction of effective racial equality.

This volume will examine how labour came to be in this position. Labour's contemporary notions of blackness and its significant field of concepts have specific conditions of emergence and were generated around frameworks set in place during the 1930s. In fact all political frameworks or grids, through which issues are accessible, are the product of past formulations, and their conditions of emergence. This means that in the 1950s and 1960s when labour was required to respond to black immigration to Britain, it drew upon frameworks from the 1930s developed to deal with anti-semitism and conceptions of blackness generated in debates about whether Indians were capable of self-government. It will be argued that labour's notions of race have significantly contributed to negative constructions of blackness, which have made their own particular contribution to racial disadvantage. This, and labour's approach to anti-racism, place in doubt its ability to act as an effective political agency in forging a form of politics which addresses black disadvantage.

Political community is a central analytical device used in this volume.[3] It is around attempts to demarcate political communities, in the context of political discourse, that notions of racial difference are brought into play. A discourse about racial difference emerges around labour's attempts to define the political community of East London in the 1930s in defending a Jewish presence. A discourse about racial difference emerges in labour's attempts to define the constituent populations making up the political community of an independent India. Some of these constructions of racial difference re-emerge during the 1950s and are recognisable in the present, in debates about immigration and nationality legislation which provide formal definitions of the British political community or nation. Political communities are collectivities of human subjects or populations with an identifiable commonality. Concepts like British, Jewish, commonwealth and black are all references to political communities construed in discourse. Political community is an important concept which organises other concepts including race. We shall return to it, adding other layers of complexity as the arguments in this volume develop.

Labour's approach to race issues occurs in a specific context:

its commitment to socialism. Conceptions of socialism, which like race are generated in discourse, are important in organising labourist notions of race and racial difference. Labourist notions of socialism (for there are many) provide a flexible framework through which other issues are sifted. This volume will show that labour has had numerous conceptions of socialism available to it, both today and in the 1930s. Issues debated within the Labour Party may be seen as competing claims to define the party's political concerns: socialism in its various forms. Some of these become official policy. Others are rejected. In analysing this process of legitimation and rejection, this volume will map out some of the political limits of labourism, and the manner in which they were sustained. Both the 1930s and the 1980s provide graphic illustration of the limits of labourism. Actions against militant supporters of recent years recall much earlier on-slaughts on communist influences. One of the most striking and enduring features of labourism is its opposition to those who challenge its constructions of socialism. This volume is as much an exploration of labour as a political agency, as it is about its conceptualisation of race.

Accounts of labour's dealings with race traditionally begin in the early 1960s and highlight the party's shocking collapse into a bipartisan consensus over the need for immigration controls in 1964. The history of this remains obscure. But labour's agreement to implement immigration controls is less surprising when placed in the context of its understanding of racial difference, and the political communities it helped to construe. Labour discourses in the 1930s were rich in racial imagery. Race was a significant form of human difference used to distinguish one population from another. Labour drew upon, and con-tributed to, notions of racial difference in articulating conceptions of political community in the 1930s which retained a significance in postwar politics. This volume explores two seminal constructions of political community by labour in the 1930s which utilise conceptions of racial difference.

The first of these political communities was India in transition from imperial domination to independent nationhood, a process in which labour was heavily involved. Racial difference was a significant concept in this context and was organised around the capacity for citizenship. Citizenship capacity was a way of

4

referring to a series of other capacities such as industriousness, orderliness and so on. Many capacities re-emerge as significant in the 1960s and 1970s when labour was confronted with the presence of black immigrants in Britain. Labour's second political community emerged around its response to anti-semitic agitation in East London and other large cities. Active anti-semitic agitation forced the Labour Party to say what it was defending, and against what. It was forced to articulate its notion of Jewishness which it distinguished from Britishness. These of course utilised conceptions of racial difference. At this time Britishness could not sustain the idea of a multi-racial community which incorporated visible physical difference. Jews would either assimilate or disappear to Palestine.

Labour's response to anti-semitism also provides an early example of what was later to be called anti-racism. Labour set about opposing anti-semitism in a highly qualified manner. Firstly it was not able to see anti-semitism as a specific attack on Jews, or as a form of what was later referred to as racism. Anti-semitism was seen as a feature of fascism, and Jews were simply the first in a line of victims to be followed by the labour movement and its constituency, workers. Labour was unable to defend Jews as a racially defined category of the population; it was able only to defend them as workers. Its defence of Jewish people was further limited by its understanding of democracy and public order. Labour's understanding of racism as a feature of the broader problem of fascism persisted into the late 1970s and was still in evidence in the mid-1980s. Its engagement with racist agitators today is still circumscribed by its concern for public order.

The central project of this volume is to understand why labour's approach to race has been, and continues to be, so limited, and what this means in terms of labour's potential for addressing racial disadvantage. Is labour capable of converting its conception of social justice into political and social reforms which address black disadvantage? An important step in this process would require labour to reconstruct itself as a political agency and tackle seriously the issue of black representation in the party. Labour has refused seriously to address the demand for black sections in the party. In so doing it has marginalised its own black members, their constituency and their political demands.

Whilst black representation does not guarantee an anti-racist politics, it is unacceptable that an anti-racist politics should exclude black people. Labour's conception of social justice has not so far been applied to the social inequalities suffered by black Britons. Some fundamental changes in the organisation, political priorities and constituencies of the Labour Party will be necessary if labour is ever to become a political force in addressing racial disadvantage, division and discord in British society.

1

EXPLORING RACE AND LABOURISM
A conceptual framework

This volume explores the race concept, and the nature of the
Labour Party as a political agency. It does so through the
analytical techniques of discourse analysis. This requires a
theoretical framework which needs clarification and contextualisation. This chapter considers, in turn, existing theoretical work
on race, the application of Foucauldian discourse analysis in
examining the race concept, and contemporary work on the
Labour Party.

RACE AS DISCURSIVE CONSTRUCT

Race is a concept. An abstraction. It is not a real thing, an object
perceptible to the senses. It is an idea used to distinguish and
classify human beings. Other, similar ideas, like gender, are also
used to distinguish and classify human beings. So what is unique
about race as a classificatory system? The uniqueness of race is a
central issue in the arguments developed in this volume. Case-
study material contained in documents on anti-semitism, on
India, on immigration and nationality law and on black
communities in Britain from the 1960s to the present, provide
fragments of discourses about race. They show that what is
unique to the race concept is its association in discourse with a
clustering of other concepts and objects. It is this which gives race
its distinctiveness. The first thing we may note about race is that
it is a concept which has a unique relationship to other concepts
and objects with which it is linked in political discourse.

Deconstructing the race concept begins with the identification
of its field of objects and concepts presented in discourse. Objects

7

and concepts are rather usefully distinguished by Foucault (1972: 40–9, 56–63) whose analysis can be developed to effect the following distinction. Concepts are purely abstract: they have no material existence. They are ideas used to understand and organise our material world like, for example, class. Concepts are registered in discourses, for, because they are only ideas and not things, they can exist only when they are spoken about. In being spoken about they enter the domain of discourse. Objects, on the other hand, do have a material reality. They exist in a world which is available to the senses, and do not disappear if we fail to notice them. But they are never non-discursive. As soon as we try to understand the objects around us we organise them, arrange them, and speak about them. As we do this they enter the domain of discourse, or things spoken of. Objects therefore are both discursive and non-discursive, whilst concepts are more purely discursive.

It has been suggested so far that the race concept is distinguishable by the clustering of objects it attracts when it occurs in discourse. Objects attached to the race concept are mainly ways of establishing human physical differences. Black skin and black bodies are obvious examples. But the case study on Jews in East London indicates a range of other physical attributes which have nothing to do with colour, but which are also organised by the race concept. Statements about Jews in the 1930s are peppered with references to distinctively shaped noses and heads, as visible signs of Jewishness, which recall eighteenth-century concerns with anatomy as a basis for human classification. This points to one of the few generalisations it is possible to make about race: its associated field of objects includes reference to phenotypical variation, thus claiming a basis in human anatomy.

The fact that the race concept organises a clustering of objects in which physical difference has priority is not, of course, a new discovery. As numerous writers have pointed out, for example, Husband (1984: 13), physical difference is only a sign of category membership. It is the social significance of physical difference which has attracted the intellectual energies of social scientists. Accounts of race developed within sociology and cultural studies mostly begin by referring to the inevitable relationship between phenotypical variation and social attributes. This juxtaposition of the anatomical and the social is characteristic of the human sciences. For example, Miles's (1982: 9) dismissal of race as a scientific error echoes Banton and Harwood's (1975: 8) reference to racial categorisation as 'delusionary', and serves to underline the point that racial classifications are widely regarded as social myths. Race in the human sciences is now widely regarded as a social and political construct.

This leap from race-associated objects, like phenotypical variation, to assembling the social myths surrounding the race concept has led to a vast and useful academic output on racism, but has failed to elucidate the field of concepts clustered with race in discourse, and because of this our understanding of race lacks important detail. This is important because what distinguishes the race concept is not just its association with particular objects like phenotypical variation, but its specific constellation of related concepts. Race is a concept with a particular field of related concepts which give it a particularity, and distinguish it from other concepts used to categorise populations like gender. This specificity can be more fully explored.

What are the concepts with which race is associated in political discourse? The answer to this question rather depends on the context in which racial distinctions are constructed. The case study on India, for example, shows that in discharging its colonial responsibilities organising decolonisation, the Labour Party articulated forms of racial classification drawn from comparative philology[1] and from eighteenth-century anthropology.[2] The Labour Party took these notions of race to the debates over Indian independence where they encountered new demands. These new demands required that Indians be classified into those who could, and those who could not, sustain the duties and obligations of citizenship, for the entire debate over Indian independence focused on whether Indians were capable of self-government. In using racial classifications to make these distinctions regarding citizenship, race was significantly reconstructed as a concept. Whilst race had, historically, been used to speak about human capacities such as civilisation and so on, it would in future also be used to discuss black citizenship. But citizenship is itself a concept with its own field of concepts; significantly also human capacities such as industriousness, civilisation, education, orderliness and so on. Whilst these were not newly associated with race or with citizenship they were newly brought into a discourse concerning the political capacities of peoples with black skin. As the first black British colony to become independent from Britain, India placed the issue of black self-government on labour's political agenda. This process of deconstruction of the race concept reveals the processes through which it is constructed, instead of simply asserting that race is a socially constructed category.

Untangling the field of objects and concepts activated by notions of race, in any particular period, has a further advantage. Objects and concepts can be traced back to their use in other contexts. They can be plotted as they re-emerge, dragging old imagery into new contexts. The field of concepts used to compile conceptions of racial difference in the 1930s in the context of Indian independence and anti-semitism in East London, can be traced as they re-emerge in postwar approaches to black immigration. Objects and concepts are retrieved for analysis from discourse. Cutler *et al.* (1977: 4, 10, 211) have suggested that discourse is a register of concepts. Discourse, as Cousins and Hussain (1984: 77) suggest, is now an over-used technique in the social sciences, and clarification of its use in this volume is needed.

Discourse is used by Miles (1982, 1989) and other marxist analysts of race as an investigative device to reveal a racist ideology. In Miles's (1989) detailed and scholarly work discourse is a register of ideas and thinking about race which provides clues to the bigger system of ideas, racist ideology. Discourse in this volume is not a point of access to ideology, and this account has no theory of racist ideology in the sense of its place in the overall scheme of things. Racism, like all other concepts, is given a force and meaning in the contexts in which it occurs. Although this volume shares with Miles and others the view that discourse is a register of ideas and thought, it uses discourse in a Foucauldian sense and not just to indicate that of which it is possible to speak, as Miles does. It utilises Foucault's theory of knowledge,[3] which Miles rejects, and develops Foucault's analytical framework to provide a way of understanding race.

The form of discourse analysis developed in this volume has a number of distinctive features. The first concerns the distinction between objects and concepts already outlined. Foucault's insistence that texts should be read to determine their particular arrangement of concepts and objects, prompted the observation outlined earlier, that race is a concept which organises a field of concepts and objects in discourse. But concepts and objects are not just arranged in discourses waiting to be discovered, and this points to a further distinctive feature of Foucault's analytic technique. Concepts, and their field of concepts, are generated in the discourses in which they occur. Discourse is a dynamic and relational form of analysis. The race concept emerged from the discourse on Indian decolonisation reconstructed by the requirements of that discourse which were about citizenship capacity. Foucault's analytic framework also supplies a notion of 'conditions of emergence' which is a useful device for interrogating the race concept. It makes it possible to establish the conditions in which any particular understanding of race was made possible. The idea that concepts have conditions of emergence allows us to ask, for example, what made the Labour Party's particular understanding of Jewishness in the 1930s possible. So Foucault's framework, as well as providing a means of conceptualising the generation of social categories, also allows speculation on why they took the form they did. The notion of constraint[4] provides the means of establishing conditions of emergence. Constraints are the circumstances which fashion a particular understanding of a situation. Some of the constraints producing labour's defence of the Jews in the 1930s, for example, include its understanding of European fascism as a threat to the labour movement, and a conception of socialism in which forms of economic participation were prioritised over racial or ethnic categories. These constraints made multi-racialism an impossible concept for labour in the 1930s.

Discourse analysis provides a grid in which certain questions can be posed about the arrangement and construction of objects and concepts; and about the conditions in which certain understandings of racial difference are made possible. In this volume discourse is used in two senses. It is used both to refer to a collection of statements, and to the method by which they may be analysed. It is this combination of the two meanings of discourse which distinguishes this volume from other accounts of race. The term discourse will be used throughout the book to refer to collections and forms of statement (and it should be noted that practice and actions are also forms of statement), as in 'labour discourse', but it will examine these discourses using the method outlined. This is not an attempt to be more purely Foucauldian than other analysts of race. It is merely an attempt to establish an analytical framework which reveals some features of the race concept which are not revealed in other accounts.

Discourses and their statements are constructed and registered in texts.[5] Two criteria are used in the selection of texts for analysis in this volume. Firstly, they must deal with issues which have a bearing on race, and secondly, they must have something to do with the Labour Party. Labour statements may be official policy statements, or they may occur in parliamentary debates, or newspaper articles or in conference speeches. We may also consider statements by other organisations and publications lobbying the Labour Party and attempting to define a set of political concerns on its behalf. Most of the texts examined in this book were culled from the archives of the Labour Party, the Communist Party, the Indian Nationalist Movement, and the official records of various Indian trade union organisations. Much of the material on anti-semitism comes from local Labour Party records in East London and from the Poale Zion, the Jewish Labour Party. Clearly not all statements carry equal weight, and official declarations of policy and intent are distinguished from other statements, and from political action.

The implications of this volume's distinctive use of race as a discursive construct become apparent when discussed in the context of other work on race. Contemporary accounts of race may be generally divided into the structural and the cultural. Structural refers to those accounts which generally draw on a marxist analysis, like the work of Robert Miles (1982, 1989), Miles and Phizacklea (1979a, 1979b, 1980); and those accounts which Gilroy (1987: 20) describes as operating on the boundaries of marxism and Weberianism, like the work of John Rex (1986) and Rex and Tomlinson (1979). Cultural refers to those accounts which prioritise the study of cultural forms. These investigate racism as a cultural feature of British capitalism's imperial heritage, responsible for generating its own counter-cultures of black resistance. The work of the Birmingham Centre for Contemporary Cultural Studies (1982) and Paul Gilroy (1987) are cogent examples of this genre. There are two key tension points between the theorisation of race in this volume as a concept constructed in discourse, and the theorisation of race in cultural and structural accounts. Firstly the conceptualisation of race in this volume poses no general relationship between race and class as political forces, for investigation or comment. Secondly, the conceptualisation of race offered here does not require a theory of ideology or try to provide an account of the general relationship between ideological, political and economic forms. An exploration of these tension points develops a clearer picture of the race concept offered in this volume, and locates it in terms of other contributions.

Structuralist accounts informed by a marxist perspective share with the rather more Weberian accounts of Rex, and Rex and Tomlinson, a concern to account for the social locations of black Britons through a concept of class. The articulation of race and class as forms of social division was a key theoretical issue for sociologists concerned with race in the 1970s.[6] The result was the grafting of race onto the more significant and theoretically established social division of class. Terms such as 'sub-proletariat' 'underclass' and 'racialised fraction of the working class' insist that race is a sub-division of class. Even in Miles's (1989: 134) schema, although the social significance of blackness is thoroughly and delicately construed, ultimately, the social locations of black Britons are the product of racialisation, forms of exclusion operating in a context of class relations which retain an analytic primacy. It only remains to determine the precise articulation of these processes in which classes are formed and in which racialisation occurs. There are two problems with this kind of analysis.[7] The first is its attempt to establish a permanent and general relationship between race and class. Surely this relationship is dynamic and contextual, taking different forms in different contexts? It is further assumed that class is always a more real or privileged social division, around which other divisions are organised. This prioritisation of class does not make it any more real than any other social division. Class is simply a priority constructed in discourses concerned with socialism. It acquires its analytic primacy from a set of discourses which has difficulty in prioritising other forms of social division. The second problem with marxist explanations of the relationship between race and class concerns their political implications. If class is the most significant of social divisions, then class struggles are more important than other struggles. Black struggles, in marxist discourse, are only significant if they challenge capitalism. The marginalisation of black struggles is made easier by the assumption that black and class politics are in no way contradictory, that the one supports and reinforces the other. This point is contested by Feuchtwang (1980), who argues that socialist, feminist and anti-racist struggles each have their own political objectives and may conflict with others.

The subordination of black to class politics is challenged by black marxists[8] such as Sivanandan, influential in the journal *Race and Class*, and those who study the place of black resistance in challenging cultural forms such as the Birmingham Centre for Contemporary Cultural Studies (1982). These accounts rescue black struggles from the margins of politics by insisting that struggles against racism are always struggles against capital. In this way black people become the vanguard of the revolutionary class. In a hierarchy of oppressions generated by capitalism, and understood by social scientists through the concepts race and class, the struggle against black oppression is the most fundamental of all struggles, the overthrow of capitalism. Black people, suffering multiple oppression through capitalism and racism, have a greater capacity for revolt than the working class as a whole. They are construed as a vanguard of revolutionary vanguards. This approach does not significantly re-theorise the relationship between race and class posed by Miles, but rethinks its political implications. Notions of revolt are significant in constructing blackness as a political category in this kind of approach. Whilst the analysis just offered is critical of what is at stake in these accounts, black activists are quite right to insist on the centrality of their struggles, for they have no guarantees that a general class politics will ever address their concerns, or tackle their oppression. Indeed labour's class politics has sustained and not challenged racial disadvantage.

No general analysis of the relationship between race and class is offered in this volume. In fact it contests the assumption that there is a general relationship between the social divisions invoked in using the term race, and those which are invoked in using the term class. Clearly race is a social division which confronts others in discourse. But it does so differently in different contexts. In the context of Labour Party discourses, the social divisions of race and class confront each other in a number of senses. Race and class confront each other as competing constituencies[9] and political objectives.[10] They confronted each other when sections of the Labour Party decided to support Indian nationalist activities which damaged the interests of British trade unionists in the 1930s. The foreign cloth boycott in India, which gave force to the demand for independence, was hardly in the interests of Lancashire cotton operatives. Race and class were also brought into confrontation when labour decided that Jews could only be defended from anti-semitic attacks as members of the working class, and not as Jews. In the example of Indian nationalist struggles race is given primacy over class. In the example of anti-semitism, class triumphs over race, for the Labour Party cannot admit to a racially divided constituency. These two examples show that race and class in political discourse sustain different forms of politics and are not locked into any permanent form of association. It is better to see this as a relationship constructed in specific forms in particular discourses.

Conflict between constituencies organised by the race concept and constituencies organised by a notion of class, is familiar territory in the Labour Party today. The struggles over race politics on Liverpool's Militant-dominated labour council illustrates this very point. So too, does this anecdote from a local ward meeting of the Labour Party in the London Borough of Hackney in 1987. A resolution was hastily presented to the meeting calling for support for suspended town hall trade unionists. Such a victimisation of workers, even by a labour council, is an obvious rallying point in asserting a class politics. Perhaps noticing that members of the ward's black section were sitting quietly in a row examining their shoes, a member asked why the trade unionists had been suspended. 'For racial harassment' came the hesitant reply! This illustrates the point that race and class politics are not necessarily compatible, and that what appears to be a theoretical distinction between constituencies has a force in everyday political decision-making. How to deal with the demands for an effective approach to racism in the context of a class politics is one of the dilemmas of the modern Labour Party.

The second difference between the treatment of race in this volume and in other accounts concerns the status of ideology. It was suggested earlier that most accounts of race are, quite properly, committed to identifying racism. Marxist explanations of race developed within a Gramscian framework, like that of Miles (1982, 1989), despite providing an elaborate account of racism as ideology, autonomous from capital, ultimately support the notion that capital is a determining force, fracturing the working class along racial lines. Hence the rationale for the 'racialised fraction' thesis (Miles 1982: 159). Ultimately in marxist accounts capitalism needs racist ideology to sustain itself.

Cultural accounts of race, such as Gilroy's (1987) and those of the authors of the Birmingham Centre for Contemporary Cultural Studies (1982) publication *The Empire Strikes Back*, share Miles's Gramscian framework. In *The Empire* the basic marxist framework is overlain by a Gramscian terminology which insists that state racism is 'complex', that world and nationalist capitalist processes are 'contradictory', and that the roots of racist ideology 'cannot be reduced to a simple ideological phenomenon' (1982: 9). As readers pick their way through the 'organic' and the 'hegemonic', the message is this: racism is deeply embedded in a culture of British nationalism, fashioned by colonial structures essential to the survival of British capitalism. Ultimately, this comes to the same conclusion as Miles. Racism serves the needs of British capitalism, but this time the focus is on its nationalistic and imperialistic form. But the focus of *The Empire* is quite different from that of Miles's work. In an attempt to illustrate the point that racism is embedded in capital's colonial strategy, *The Empire* treats the reader to a reconstruction of colonial histories in which the significance of colonial ideologies to a contemporary understanding of racism is never made clear. But the reconstruction of colonialism in *The Empire* is not about clarifying racism. The elaboration of a racist ideology is sacrificed to another political project altogether. *The Empire* is an attempt to construct, historically, a black constituency around its capacity to resist colonialism and slavery, for it is this which empowers a black constituency to resist contemporary racism (Knowles and Mercer 1990: 72). But the racism to be resisted takes second place to the need to assert a black identity in struggle. This is a very important point, but the lack of a well developed notion of racism in this account leaves it without a precise target against which to mobilise its constituency. It is fair to ask of this kind of account:

16

Having constructed a black constituency, what do you propose to mobilise it against? For state power and capitalism make rather vague enemies.

Gilroy's (1987) work presents a similar problem. It conveys, quite properly, a general deference to the 1980s uprisings, but does so without questioning the political objectives or outcomes of these struggles. Clearly they are legitimate expressions of anger and frustration. But do they provide the political impetus to address black disadvantage? Or do they aid the destruction and pathologisation of black communities? Black civil rights are, in fact, lost in a rhetoric which insists on a black vanguard launching itself at any target, the state, the local state, capitalism in general, employers and so on. All black struggles, Gilroy implies, are equally valid and are unquestioningly presented as struggles against racism, and hence capitalism. The challenges of the 1990s require a more detailed analysis than this. But can a framework which asserts the inevitability of black oppression sustain a detailed programme of reforms?

Like other accounts, this volume is about racism. It is about the construction of race and racism as political categories. But racism does not necessarily require a theory of ideology or a general theory of the relationship between ideology, politics and economic forces. Racism, like race, is a concept constructed in specific discourses. It has a related field of objects and concepts upon which it draws, and which can be identified. This study is concerned to identify labour conceptions of racism and the means by which it may be addressed, anti-racism. Racism is whatever it is claimed to be in discourse. In the case study of anti-semitism, for example, racism is constructed in terms of physical attacks on Jews, antagonistic propoganda and so on. Racism has a related field of objects which have an existence outside discourse. These may include social practices, official procedures, or seemingly irrational actions by individuals like setting fire to Jewish or Asian homes. But labour's conception of racism is also being judged in this study. Does it, for instance, damage or disadvantage black people? Racism is also a matter of effect (Feuchtwang 1982: 251). This volume will demonstrate that labour's constructions of race and racism, and its use of these concepts in distinguishing a political community of black subjects, itself sustains, and gives political direction to, racial inequality. The understanding of racism offered in this volume, that it is a concept constructed in discourse, and a range of discursive and extra-discursive practices which have the effect of generating or sustaining (or in some way contributing to) black disadvantage, requires no theory of ideology or an account of the relationship between ideology and capitalism. Whilst racism is not disconnected from British capitalism the association between the two remains to be determined in specific contexts.

LABOURISM

Understanding race and racism as concepts constructed in labour discourse requires an analysis of labourism. The term labourism has a sub-text. It is dismissive and hints at betrayal. Coates (1982: 135) quotes with satisfaction the view of Saville that '. . . labourism has nothing to do with socialism'. Labourism is a label used to refer to what the Labour Party stands for, and to stake out an opposition between this and socialism. Labourism is a cryptic way of referring to labour's betrayal of socialism. For socialism, constructed within a marxist framework, demands a class analysis of society, and a commitment to revolutionary, or at least radical, change. Labourism is used as a motif. It indexes labour's failure properly to represent the interests of its legitimate constituency, the working class, and characterises much that has been written about the party.

This is not the sense in which the concept labourism is used in this study. Labourism is a way of referring to the range of political processes and conceptualisations which occur within a set of political boundaries. Labourism in this volume is simply a way of referring to all that takes place within the boundaries of the Labour Party and is accessible through case studies. Labour's discourse on race reveals as much about labourism as it does about race. Labourism, in this volume, is a cryptic way of referring to a politics constructed within and around the Labour Party, and available for analysis through the party's documentation and actions.

Some central features of labourism are construed in the party's constitution. This defines the political space in which it operates, its potential membership, political orientation, organisational structure and strategies. Eligibility for party membership is still tied to eligibility for trade union membership.

It is this stipulation which gives labour its distinctive claim to speak on behalf of the labour movement, and is an important reference point in staking out labourism. This stipulation also explains labour's policy orientation, heavily weighted towards a trade union stance, at the expense of broader political objectives. Labour members are formally bound to act within the constitution and abide by the policy and standing orders of the party. Because of its strategic importance in defining the Labour Party, the constitution has always been a site of struggle for competing definitions of the party and its political priorities.

The Labour Party is also construed through its central political objectives. These are bounded by four general reference points which have the effect of constraints. These remain the same today as in the 1930s, and establish the general political space within which labour operates. The first of these constraints establishing the general parameters of labourism, is a commitment to working through the parliamentary system. One of the most significant features of labourism, this circumscribes labour's mode of political intervention and available strategies. The second constraint concerns labour's links with trade unionism, also insisted upon as a condition of membership, and establishes an underlying commitment to a particular kind of politics. The third constraint concerns labour's constituency. Labourism is constitutionally concerned with the representation of 'workers by hand or by brain' in the task of securing a 'common ownership of the means of production' as well as 'emancipation of the people' (Labour Party 1929: 3 and 1985a: 288). Finally there is also a commitment by labour to securing international co-operation. Because labour's political objectives are about trade unionism, parliamentary democracy and workers (all domestic issues) it has always had enormous difficulty in developing a distinctive foreign policy.

Within these political boundaries labourism is eclectic. Within labour's constitutionally defined political space exists a diversity of competing and contradictory policies, statements, principles and actions. An examination of any issue demonstrates the party's political diversity. For example, debates over Indian independence in the 1930s reveal a spectrum of political positions ranging from the view that India should immediately and unreservedly be granted independence, to the view that

19

Indians were permanently incapable of self-government. Similarly today, there are those in the Labour Party who still want strict immigration controls and those who argue that there should be none at all. Labour is patently capable of great political diversity. But what does this tell us about the party? If, as this volume suggests, the Labour Party is not simply a monument to be described, but is actively constructed through the political discourse with which it engages, then differing political positions must be seen as competing claims to define the party itself through its political concerns. The Labour Party may be a political institution, but it is also a discursive concept. It could not exist without formally constituting itself and the act of constitution forces labour into the domain of discourse. Clues as to the nature of labour as a political agency are therefore embedded in all of its forms of statement, collectively referred to as labour discourse. Through the discourse it is possible to map the limits of labourism by establishing the range of political positions tolerated by labour. But not all positions carry equal weight, and it is also possible to map official labourism: those positions which carry the weight of sanction from the central enunciative sites in the party. In order to be acceptable as official policy, political positions must meet certain requirements, or conditions of authorisation. In general, conditions of authorisation require a statement of orderly political conduct and a respect for a certain kind of democratic process (National Executive Committee 1933).

Despite its eclecticism labourism has a set of political boundaries. There are positions which are excluded, and others which are tolerated. Mapping the political boundaries of labourism is one of the tasks of this study. Political boundaries are established through exclusion. Some political forces in the party are kept under greater surveillance than others. For example, labour historically keeps a close watch on its youth wing, which it has always suspected of communist, and latterly Trotskyist, sympathies. Exclusion from the Labour Party usually occurs on constitutional grounds. The Labour Party, it seems, has never expelled anyone for their political views; even Oswald Mosley was expelled only for breaching the party constitution and standing orders. Concerns for constitutionality, however, serve other concerns, acting as a defence against alternative definitions of socialism. Labourism is centrally concerned with socialism.

The Labour Party's policy review exercises of the late 1980s, in declaring 'We are democratic socialists', recall the 1920s and 1930s when successive conferences declared the party's commitment to socialism (1988: 2). Socialism, like labourism, is a concept constructed in discourse and has many meanings. But socialism is something which labour shares with other political groups who proffer alternative conceptions. Labourist notions of socialism, therefore, need to be defended.

Understanding labour's relation to socialism is most effectively achieved in the context of some of the more prominent accounts of the Labour Party. Definitions of socialism and of labourism are, for example, offered by prominent historians of the Labour Party. The work of G.D.H. Cole (1969), Ralph Miliband (1975) and Ben Pimlott (1977) offer competing conceptions of socialism and of the political significance of the Labour Party. Their focus assesses labour's capacity for socialism, and their work is indicative of much else that has been written about labour. Each of these accounts presents significant moments in labour history designed to address the question: Was the Labour Party (and hence can it ever be) a force for social justice? Each account has its own definition of socialism and social justice, and its own account of whose interests are served by labour. For Miliband and Pimlott the history of the Labour Party is a history of failure. Cole was more optimistic and provides a more detailed history. For Pimlott, labour failed to grasp the opportunity to make limited reforms which would have improved working class living standards. For Miliband, labour's failure lay in its reluctance to organise the latent spirit of working class revolution. For him the history of the party is one of missed opportunity – the general strike of 1926, the insurrectionary mood of 1919 and so on. These accounts provide the basic framework of issues raised in later accounts such as those in the journal *New Left Review*. It is here that the dichotomy between socialism and labourism is staked out anew. Coates (1982: 54) insists that the Labour Party is 'not a suitable vehicle for the pursuit of socialism'. Hoare and Ali (1982) state a similar position in the context of deciding whether socialists should organise inside or outside the Labour Party. Wainwright (1987) too considers this same issue in exploring the 'Limits of Labourism', more accurately described as a statement of the limitations of

21

labourism. These are all important assessments of whether the Labour Party is capable of becoming a force for social reconstruction. But in the context of much of the work in *New Left Review*, this is not a genuine question. It is instead an opportunity to restate with new and mounting evidence the distance between real socialism and the pathetic efforts of the Labour Party.

The account of labourism provided in this volume is not intended as a contrast to socialism. Labourism in this study refers to a set of political positions and a mode of political engagement, the salient features of which have already been outlined. It is apparent that labourism is constructed around certain kinds of political concerns and strategies. Labourism, in all of its diversity, defines its political concerns with some reference to socialism. Socialism is a key reference point in constructing labourism, and stands for whatever is claimed on its behalf in discourse. As in the accounts of *New Left Review*, labour in this study is also being judged as a political agency offering social justice. But concerns with social justice in this volume are concerns for racial inequality, and socialism is only relevant in so far as it provides a framework for labourism.

The Foucauldian discourse analysis used in this study is particularly suited to the analysis of political institutions and processes. It provides a language and a conceptual grid which is appropriate to this purpose. It allows, for example, an understanding of the Labour Party as an enunciative site, comprising other enunciative sites like the national executive, the parliamentary party, the youth wing, policy committees and so on. The Foucauldian concepts of voice and constituency also have an analytic purchase in helping to distinguishing whom the Labour Party may be representing in any particular statement. Numerous political voices are articulated from within labour's ranks. These may be identified in terms of their political objectives and their constituencies. Who is speaking? And what are their political demands?

LABOUR AND RACE

Accounts of the Labour Party which involve an interrogation of socialism, like Miliband's, Pimlott's, Cole's and those which feature in *New Left Review*, all share a disinterest in race issues.

Race is excluded from most general accounts of the nature of labourism, and this reflects the marginalisation of race as an issue in labour politics, and its exclusion from assessments of labour's capacity for social justice. Whilst there is no shortage of academic work examining the relationship between the Labour Party and race issues, this work all occurs within a particular context, focused most usually on immigration, and does not tackle the character of labourism itself. Academic work on the Labour Party and race issues is characterised by three contextual features.[11] Firstly it is primarily focused on legislative forms of exclusion, immigration and its forms of redress through race relations laws. Secondly it usually discusses these issues in the context of a betrayal thesis, advancing the view that labour betrayed black Britons in changing its policy on immmigration control in 1964 (Moore 1975: 28). Thirdly the historical encounter between the Labour Party and race rarely extends further back than the early 1960s with the exception of some accounts of anti-semitism. Mesbahuddin (1987) gives a detailed account of the involvement of the Labour Party in Indian independence, but not in order to establish its early approaches to race.

Labour's race relations and immigration policy[12] are obviously of central importance. These are key issues in Paul Foot's (1965) account, and in the accounts of Moore and Wallace (1975) and Anwar (1986). There is a good deal of justifiable anger about labour's failure to implement effective race relations legislation, which could be used to challenge black disadvantage. Clearly it is unacceptable for a party concerned with social justice to implement immigration legislation which discriminates against black immigrants and their families, and academic writing correctly concerns itself with these issues. But this focus on immigration and race relations provides little context through examining labour's treatment of other race issues. This study offers a broader and more historical perspective than much existing work. Whilst it examines some of the implications of immigration, nationality and race relations legislation, it does so in order to grasp the ways in which black communities in Britian are constructed in labourist discourse. It is more interested in the construction of political categories. What is at stake in the term immigrant? How is it construed in labourist discourse, and what are its implications?

Accounts of labour's dealings with race issues are usually located in the early 1960s and focus on what is often described as the volte-face of 1964 when official Labour Party policy collapsed into a bipartisan consensus on the need to restrict immigration to Britain (Ben-Tovim *et al.* 1986: 15–16, Foot 1965: 75, Moore 1975: 25). But labour has a history of dealing with race which goes back before the 1960s (Solomos 1989). As this study demonstrates, labour's dealings with postwar race issues have some definite conditions of emergence in the 1930s debates over Indian independence and anti-semitism. Once it is understood that labourist constructions of the significance of racial difference in postwar politics drew upon these 1930s conceptions, it should come as no surprise that labour agreed to immigration controls in 1964.

Labour's dealings with race are also frequently presented as betrayals. This thesis is partly the result of the events of 1964 which were interpreted as a major about-turn in labour thinking, and partly derived from a marxist interpretation of the Labour Party's acts of class betrayal. If, so the argument goes, capitalism requires racism, and the Labour Party is a political agency rooted in capitalist relations of production, then it is not surprising that it behaves in ways which disadvantage black peoples. An account of labour and race which appears to reject this understanding and then, later, collapses into it is that of Ben-Tovim *et al.* (1986): an excellent detailed study of race politics in Liverpool and Wolverhampton. This seems to reject the classic marxist alignment between the Labour Party, social democracy, capitalism and racism. It is a serious attempt to understand how racism is constructed in local politics and insists that the conditions in which labour generates racism are open to challenge. Ultimately, however, this book retains the concepts ideology and state, though admittedly in a disaggregated sense, and institutional racism as a grim inevitability. What is identified by Ben-Tovim *et al.* (1986: 73) as positive anti-racist moves by local labour parties 'betray a deep seated resistance to the development of anti-racist policies'. If this is the case then labour will always betray black people. It would be helpful to know how this deep seated resistance is produced and sustained in labour politics.

24

CONCLUSION

This study begins to address some of these issues in plotting the emergence of race in labourist politics and examining the manner in which political categories like race, racism and anti-racism are generated and sustained. It also speculates about the likelihood that labour could become an agency for an anti-racist politics and what this might involve. There is nothing inevitable about labour's approach to race. It was constructed in the first place, and it is constantly being reconstructed. Race politics is a process.

2

SOCIALISM IN THE 1930s AND FOR THE 1990s

It was argued in chapter one that socialism is a concept constructed in discourse, and a central political commitment for labour. It was also argued that labourism sustains a range of conceptions of socialism, which compete to define the party's political priorities, and that this provides a grid through which issues like race are sifted. This chapter documents some of labour's conceptions of socialism. It does so in order to detail the content and limits of labourism, and hence to establish the distinctiveness of labour as a political agency. The competing conceptions of socialism which constitute labourism are analysed on three interconnected levels: policy, the philosophical under-pinnings of policy, and labour's institutional boundaries. In exploring labour's institutional boundaries we are drawn into an account of how labour operates as a political party, its enunci-ative sites and the conditions of authorisation of political statement.

The early 1930s and the late 1980s provide two case studies of labourist constructions of socialism. Their political circumstances are, of course, quite different. The political landscape of the 1980s has been sculpted by a particular brand of conservatism in the Thatcher era. During this the Labour Party has reconstructed itself through changes in party organisation, through a more extensively democractic process in the re-selection of MPs, and through its methods of leadership selection. Labour has also reconstructed its conceptions of socialism through its policy review process of the late 1980s, which may be seen as an attempt to up-date socialism. A rather similar process of introspection occurred in the 1930s, when labour was also condemned to a long period as the parliamentary opposition. It was in the 1930s that labour developed, for the first time, an elaborate structure of policy-making through committees. It was through these committees that labour was able to convert its notions of socialism into policy detail, providing the means of government for the 1945 labour administration. The 1930s were a productive period for labour in which it fashioned a political alternative to conservatism and liberalism. A good deal of progress was made, in the 1930s period of introspection, in the task of creating a political agency with a policy-making machinery, which could successfully offer itself to an electorate. In fact labourism was only fully created in the 1930s.

SOCIALIST POLICY IN THE 1930s

Labour policy definitions[1] of socialism in the 1930s reveal a tension between social welfare and industrial reconstruction as political concerns. This is demonstrated in the struggle between George Lansbury and Stafford Cripps. Should welfare reforms, referred to by Cripps (1932: 286) as 'ambulance work', or a new policy outlining industrial reconstruction, be labour's priority? These two positions may be seen as competing attempts to define proper socialist concerns, and a suitable image for the Labour Party. Stafford Cripps's plea for industrial reconstruction was the focus for a lively debate about the most appropriate form of public ownership. Public ownership was at the centre of labour's industrial strategy in the 1930s; it was about the extent of state control over key industries and services.[2] Should state control be extended to banking and financial services in order to avoid sabotage by capitalist interests as Cole (1931: 1) suggests?[3] Or was it also necessary to restructure government processes to avoid defeat in the House of Lords, as Cripps (1933: 160) himself claimed? This debate about the nature of socialism was also a bid to define the party's priority constituency. Should labour prioritise workers and trade unionists, or the poor in need of welfare benefits? Lansbury's claim was furthering the interests of the poor, the dispossessed and disabled. This social work and methodist-inspired[4] tradition of labourism was dismissed by Cripps (1932: 286) as the politics of the 'underdog', and an unsuitable political image. Cripps and Bevin (Bullock 1960: 425) insisted on labour prioritising trade union interests in a policy of

27

industrial reorganisation. Finally, Cripps's claims were successful in terms of establishing labour's priorities, but Lansbury's concerns remained a central labourist theme.

As suggested above, the Labour Party was confronted with a number of political possibilities in defining itself, and the cause of socialism, in the early 1930s. A number of labourisms were on offer. How did debates about the shape of public ownership feature when presented at the level of official policy statement? Notions of public ownership which required radical political and financial reconstruction were excluded. The Labour Party's (1933a) major policy statement for the early 1930s, set out a limited programme of nationalisation of key industries, leaving financial and parliamentary structures unchanged and unchallenged. In practice then, policy definitions of socialism were even more constrained than in policy declaration. When it came to drafting legislation, labour's conceptions of socialism become even more restricted. Labour's London Passenger Transport Bill (1930), its chance to put policy definitions of socialism into practice, simply followed the liberal strategy for the coal industry. It failed, for example, to introduce any of the forms of worker participation suggested by G.D.H. Cole and the Guild Socialists.[5] The processes by which an eclectic range of stated socialisms are converted into a single legislative form is explored later in this chapter in reviewing how the Labour Party operates as an enunciative site.

SOCIALIST PHILOSOPHY IN THE 1930s

Debates about democracy were a key reference point in staking out labour's conceptions of socialism in the 1930s. Democracy is a concept which, like socialism itself, has a variety of meanings. It was often used to mark labour's political differences with the Communist Party which also made claims upon socialism as a political identity, making it important for labour to be precise about its own conceptions of socialism. Labourist notions of democracy were frequently used to distinguish labour from the Communist Party and were hence staked out against the communist antithesis, totalitarianism. Totalitarian socialism was not uncharacteristically presented in labourist discourse in terms such as 'barbarism', 'hatred' and 'terror' (Durbin 1940: 151), locating communist constructions of socialism as the expression of baser human emotions, thought indicative of a more poorly developed form of political will. This interpretation of communism was bound up with labour's reading of what was happening in the Soviet Union.[6] The conflict between democracy and totalitarianism was signified in labour's official response to Jewish defence in East London.

Conceptions of democracy, like policies on nationalisation, were also a site of struggle over the right to define the Labour Party and its political priorities. There were two seminal and conflicting conceptions of democracy advanced from within the Labour Party in the 1930s by two of its leading theorists, Evan Durbin and G.D.H. Cole. Durbin was a prolific writer on the subject of democracy and a close political associate of Keynes in the New Fabian Research Bureau (see note 3). Durbin's conception of democracy was close to the classic formulations of Mill. Because this classic formulation of democracy, revolving around parliamentary process, was something shared with other political parties, labour needed to make its claims on democratic process distinctive. It did so by attaching it to socialism. Hence, for Durbin (1935: 379), democracy was a set of political processes operating through parliament which, with proper political direction, could secure a measure of social justice. Social justice was to come through a more equitable distribution of social resources, income and property, combined with a measure of economic efficiency. Democracy for Durbin (1940: 151) was not just a superior set of political processes, it was the property of a people, a set of human capacities, the psychological disposition of a nation. A nation and its human subjects must possess the capacity for democracy, before democracy could be successfully established. Democracy was seen as the most developed form of human political organisation, demanding the most advanced of human capacities. Durbin's notion of democracy as human capacity was evident in debates concerning India's readiness for independence. Labour's commitment to awarding independent citizenship to India was construed around a discourse concerning human capacity for the democratic process. Durbin's view of democracy is very close to that which became official party policy, applied to a range of political issues and constraining official notions of political strategy.

Cole challenged Durbin's conception of democracy on behalf

of organised labour, the Labour Party's priority constituency. Cole's (1961: 454) conception of democracy was less narrowly focused on parliamentary process than Durbin's. Cole supported wider forms of public participation than were possible through parliament. For Cole (1961: 25), democracy was more than a question of political rights, it concerned the organisation of the working day. Cole advocated a form of functional representation at the point of production, with workers taking decisions about production and management. Workers were a priority constituency, and industrial participation was a form of citizenship. This conception of democracy, like Durbin's, found its way into the debates around Indian indepdendence. Worker citizenship was indeed awarded to Indian workers, though not in the form advocated by Cole. Cole's conceptualisation of democracy was intended as a critique of the Webbs and others he identified as social democrats, and shows that there were conceptions of democracy other than Durbin's available to the Labour Party in the 1930s. If labour had adopted this conception of democracy in place of Durbin's, the history of social democratic politics in Britain might have been quite different.

Because labourism is a set of discourses characterised by concerns about production, distribution, public ownership and democracy, all of which are essentially national concerns, the Labour Party has always found international policy problematic (Woolf 1947: 5–6). What might a socialist foreign policy look like? This area of policy, like others, was contested. Essentially official foreign policy was construed around two principles: the need for international co-operation, and peace.[7] These concerns became abbreviated into membership of the League of Nations and of the Labour and Socialist International. Membership of these two international organisations was a rather general commitment to international co-operation, which Labour believed to be the best guarantee of peace. This restricted conception of internationalism was not imposed by necessity. Leonard Woolf[8] developed labour's foreign and colonial policy through its policy committee structure in enormous detail. As an ex-colonial administrator Woolf (1967) had an excellent, practical grasp of colonial issues unparalleled elsewhere in the party, though these rarely found their way into official statements which remained vague and general on the matter of international relations.

Reconciling socialism with empire was not an easy task. Because this receives detailed treatment later in this volume, only one or two general points will be made here. The first point is that empire was a subject of enormous disagreement. Positions voiced from within the Labour Party on the subject of the Indian empire, for example, ranged from calls for immediate independence, to the view that the empire was better left intact. Those who maintained that the empire should remain, either believed that India was incapable of self-determination, or that it was better in socialist hands, than in being handed over to an Indian political elite, or to a greedy and inexperienced nationalist movement. In the political space between these opposed visions of empire, labour constructed an official policy, set out in 'Labour and the Nation' (Labour Party 1928). This depicted socialism's empire in terms of a commitment to the well-being of colonial subjects, the transformation of a peasant population into an industrial labour force, and the need to recognise as legitimate the demands made by colonies for independence. This official statement leads the way to the second general point about labour's empire. The empire must be industrialised. Labour found it easier to apply its conceptions of socialism to an industrial workforce than to a peasantry.

LABOUR AS AN ENUNCIATIVE SITE IN THE 1930s

Labour was, and of course still is, a single enunciative site containing other enunciative sites. Labour's key site, with the right to define party policy, was its annual party conference. Between conferences policy could be defined by the National Executive Committee (NEC). Although quite differently constituted, there was a remarkable convergence between conference and the executive, in terms of their conditions of authorisation of statements. This is evidence, if it were needed, that conference was dominated by the national executive. Because of their relationship to authorisation, both the party conference and the national executive were and are strategic enunciative sites in the party. Hence their composition, membership and access to the right to speak within them have always been sites of struggle. The authorisation of statements is important in the process of generating policy. What are these conditions of authorisation? What features does a statement need to have in order to stand a chance of becoming official party policy? An examination of official party statements reveals the following general guidelines. Firstly, a crucial factor is the extent to which statements can be linked with past statements so that there is an apparent continuity in policy and action. It is important that the present becomes a fulfilment of the past, or at least has a demonstrable link with the past. Secondly, certain standards of political strategy must be met for a statement to be authorised as official. These involve a commitment to co-operation and negotiation, rather than conflict and violence (NEC 1933).[9]

Other key enunciative sites within the party in the 1930s were the Parliamentary Labour Party and the National Joint Council. The parliamentary party has always had a difficult relationship with the national executive and party conferences, over the right to speak on behalf of the party. The parliamentary party claims a unique position in that it must both represent party policy in parliament, and discharge its representative responsibilities towards those of whom it is the elected representative. The National Joint Council comprises representatives from the parliamentary party, the Trades Union Congress and the NEC. It was formed with the aim of producing a single voice[10] for the labour movement, though in practice it has always been trade union dominated. These enunciative sites are all very public, but only policy articulated by the NEC or through successful conference resolutions are actually official; though of course a parliamentary statement carries a great deal of weight. The distinction between official and unofficial statements is an important one. Official statements carry more weight and are closer to practice, but an examination of unofficial statements gives a better indication of the limits of labourism.

THE LIMITS OF LABOURISM IN THE 1930s

There were limits to labour's eclecticism, and labour has always used its disciplinary mechanisms to operationalise a set of political boundaries and distinguish labour from non-labour positions. Whom has labour excluded from its ranks, and on what grounds? This is a way of asking what sorts of political positions labour could not tolerate. What were its boundaries as a political agency in the 1930s? What follows is a brief description of some of labour's most prominent 1930s exclusions, which provide some clues as to the limits of labourism. The labour nationalists were expelled in 1931[11] on the grounds that by joining the National Government, which was prepared to cut welfare benefits to the unemployed, they had betrayed the labour movement. In this instance the boundaries of labourism could not include such a direct attack on the living standards of labour's constituency. Oswald Mosley, an important contributor to labour policy in the 1920s, was not expelled because he was in the process of creating a political force in establishing the New Party (1931) which, when later formed into the British Union, was to become a key exponent of British fascism, but he was expelled because he had stood against the Labour Party in elections, hence breaching labour's constitution. It was not uncommon for labour to draw political boundaries around constitutional rather than political principles, so that labour never actually stated its political objections to Mosley, as it did to the labour nationalists.

Breaches of constitutional principle were often a cryptic way of referring to other, political, differences, as the expulsion of the affiliated Independent Labour Party in 1932 demonstrates.

The Independent Labour Party was expelled when it refused to take the labour whip and demanded the right to criticise the Labour Party on public platforms. This demand for a separate voice, capable of articulating non-labour positions, was a calculated assault on labour's constitution and standing orders. What was it that the Independent Labour Party wanted to say that would make it so difficult for the Labour Party to continue to absorb it? It is here that some of the discursive boundaries of labourism again become apparent. The Independent Labour Party wanted to distinguish itself from labour[12] through a commitment to mass organisation and struggle and a speedier trip down the parliamentary road to socialism than labour was prepared to entertain. This amounted to a commitment to political processes and strategies which implied conflict and worker-led action outside parliament (Brockway 1928, 1931, 1932). It over-stepped the boundaries of labourism and the Independent Labour Party went its own way into political obscurity.[13]

Curtailing the activities of its own youth wing was a common event in labour history. The League of Labour Youth, as it was known in the 1930s, made a series of political demands on its parent party which led to it being disbanded in 1936. The league sought to extend its political autonomy within the Labour Party by raising the upper age limit for league membership. The higher the age limit, the better the league was able to offer a political alternative to its parent party. The league also demanded the right to formulate its own policy outside the jurisdiction of party conference, thus giving it a separate voice. The league was finally disbanded when it used its newly won autonomy to join a united front of youth organisations, a broad anti-fascist alliance which labour suspected of communist allegiances. The suspicion of communist association, like the breaches of labour's constitution, was a shorthand way of referring to political differences which often remained unstated.

Labour's objections to the Communist Party were, however, set out in various documents.[14] The Communist Party and its members were deemed ineligible for membership of the Labour Party by the 1929 constitution, such an important political principle that it was enshrined in labour's statement of its own foundations as a political party. Its objections were threefold. First was the Communist Party's association with what was regarded as the totalitarian regime in Moscow, the antithesis of the democracy for which labour stood. Second, the Communist Party was presented as an agent of Moscow, and hence a source of internal disruption in the British labour movement. Finally, labour objected to the Communist Party's industrial strategy and its commitment to industrial conflict, in place of what were regarded as the proper methods of industrial conciliation. Labour's objections to the Communist Party extended to organisations it considered to be communist dominated. Throughout the 1930s labour issued lists of these organisations deemed ineligible for membership of the Labour Party by their communist sympathies. These lists were known as the black circulars. Their function was to police the discursive limits of labourism.

SOCIALIST POLICY FOR THE 1980s AND 1990s

Labour has recast itself, and its conceptions of socialism, in some significant respects, but it is a living statement of its own history. The discourses and processes which make up labourism today are the product of past discourses and processes, and will in turn produce the labourism of the next century. The shape of labourism for the 1990s was established through the policy review exercises of the late 1980s, the most detailed statement of which is the Labour Party's (1989) 'Meet the Challenge, Make the Change. A New Agenda for Britain'.[15] This bears the imprint of the 1930s, the Thatcher years and all that has happened between. As the filter through which labour addresses issues of race, any calculation of political outcomes around race in the 1990s must take into account current notions of socialism.

Official labourist notions of socialism developed for the 1990s have given strategic prominence to a field of concepts which are indicative of some important shifts in British politics during the Thatcher years. For example, the policy review's construction of socialism no longer prioritises state control. Socialism for the 1990s requires an economic policy which operates between the 'free market' and the 'developmental', as opposed to regulatory, role of government, using a Japanese model (Labour Party 1989: 10). What is of interest here is the transformation of government from provider to enabler, and labour's attachment to the market. Whilst the market is not a new concept in labour discourse, it is given a new prominence, marking the imprint of the Thatcher years in recasting political discourse in Britain. Competition and wealth creation provide further examples of concepts given a new prominence in labourist constructions of socialism for the 1990s. The policy review report states that a socialist economic policy 'aims to make Britain internationally competitive' and that socialism must create an economic context in which 'wealth creation' can flourish (Labour Party 1989: 9). This too indicates some important shifts in political thinking, at least in terms of political emphasis. The context in which competition and wealth are placed, however, is rather more familiar. The review subscribes to the 1930s ideas of international co-operation and social justice, through a fairer distribution of the wealth throughout the political community. Some of the more striking features of labour's reconstruction of socialism to emerge from

35

the policy review concern the role of the state in welfare provision, and in the process of industrial reconstruction. This, in turn, produces some conceptions of political community which contain some familiar (as in the case of trade unionists) and some less familiar (as in the case of women) priority constituencies.

Industrial reconstruction retains the centrality it had in the 1930s, and is contextualised by a distinctive field of concepts, notably modernisation and progress. Industrial progress has been disentangled from welfare provision, to which it was counterposed in the 1930s, and retains a central place in official definitions of socialism for the 1990s. Its field of concepts comprise 'productive', 'competitive', 'technology', 'flexibility' and 'innovation' (Labour Party 1989: 9). These concepts convey a sense of state-of-the-art production which is efficient at the job of wealth creation, and is at the heart of labourist conceptions of modern Britain. Labour's modern Britain, created through the 'leading edge of technology' and the 'importance of science' will become the 'information society' (Labour Party 1989: 12). This suggests that the creation of wealth in Britain will occur through productive, and not finance, capital. Labour believes this will, through some mechanism which ensures social justice, raise living standards. Industrial reconstruction, we are told, requires a modernised and highly trained workforce to be created through training programmes. Labour's stated commitment to equal opportunity, of course, requires the inclusion of black Britons in this, though no measures are set out to deal specifically with racial disadvantage in this area.

The state acquires a new role in industrial enterprise through industrial reconstruction. Public ownership emerges from the policy review in a partnership with industry, as the old distinction between public and private becomes 'no longer as possible or as necessary' (Labour Party 1989: 6). As public and private forms of ownership are no longer viewed as political alternatives, the state loses its regulatory and custodial role, and embraces the private sector. Gone for ever are the 'Morrisonian forms of public ownership' (Labour Party 1988: 5) which formed the flagship of 1930s socialism. These are to be replaced by a new partnership between government and industry, in which government has a developmental, and not a regulatory, role. Even the newly priva-tised public utilities such as gas, electricity and telecommunications

36

are not to be re-nationalised, but will become public interest companies under the direction of a plurality of interests, and not just government. This declining significance of the state is also evident in accounts of welfare. Welfare is a minor issue in a statement about socialism which prioritises economic and industrial policy. 'We are the party for industry' (Labour Party 1989: 6). The 'democratic and enabling state' (Labour Party 1989: 8) is constructed in terms of economic and industrial progress rather than welfare issues. The review's discussion of welfare consists of a discussion of poverty. Labour's concern with poverty is a concern for 'social justice' (Labour Party 1989: 29) and this is contingent upon economic efficiency and wealth creation. The elimination of poverty is, therefore, a subsidiary political demand to wealth creation. Poverty, which is contextualised by the review as female (but not black) is not to be addressed by a welfare state, but a 'new social insurance scheme which can meet the challenges of the 1990s . . .' (Labour Party 1989: 29). This social insurance scheme would be designed to counter the worst effects of poverty in old age, unemployment, ill-health, child-bearing, child-rearing and disability. Whilst any social insurance scheme envisaged is presumably guaranteed by the state, it is not referred to as a welfare state. References to social resources such as health and housing are, in fact, dealt with under the more general heading of consumption. Social resources are now just items of consumption along with others.[16]

The decline of the state is, of course, contested by alternative visions of socialism. The most prominent of these is associated with Eric Heffer and Tony Benn and coincides with their assault on the leadership of Neil Kinnock in the late 1980s. Benn and Heffer's (1988: 9) notion of socialism maintains labour's traditional commitment to state ownership, state economic planning and state direction of the private sector. The state maintains its centrality to socialism. It extends its functions to include the 1930s call for state control over banks and financial institutions, major companies and land for housing. This vision of socialism requires the re-nationalisation of assets privatised in the 1980s, and the kind of worker participation in production which was mooted in the 1930s by the guild socialists, but never implemented. Benn and Heffer's notion of socialism is, in many ways, a political dinosaur which vividly recalls the 1930s.

SOCIALIST PHILOSOPHY FOR THE 1980s AND 1990s

Democracy is still an important philosophical reference point in labourist constructions of socialism. Like industrial reconstruction, it is a site of struggle for competing visions of labourism. Labour's policy review conceptualises democracy as public participation, at work, in local communities and in consumption, giving people a say in all areas of their lives. It is an attempt to ensure that forms of provision are responsive to the needs of the population. Democracy in the review is participative, and not just reliant on more conventional notions of parliamentary process. 'Choice', 'rights' and a 'more equal distribution of power' (Labour Party 1989: 55) are some of the key concepts to emerge in labour's rethinking of democracy. Social justice, it seems, now requires new democratic processes. (This has a number of important implications for notions of citizenship and community which will be reviewed later.) This, labour's official conception of democracy, is also contested by Benn and Heffer's vision of socialism. The democracy envisaged by Benn and Heffer is more narrowly constructed around worker's rights and political strategies which focus on change through struggle and conflict. For Benn and Heffer democracy is about 'real struggles' (1986: 64), forms of action by industrial workers: a class, defending their interests against employers and government. This view of democracy constructs a citizenship through industrial participation in a manner which recalls guild socialism. Benn and Heffer's conception of democracy and that of the policy review is contested by 'Charter 88' which is demanding a more thorough and explicitly stated form of citizenship.[17]

Charter 88 was a demand for the modernisation of electoral and government processes, in order to make them more open, accountable, enabling of political change and more effective in the task of representing the British electorate. The charter's call for a bill of rights to ensure basic civil liberties and a modernised parliamentary democracy, is a response to the erosion of civil freedoms and increasingly centralised forms of government. Rustin (1989: 40) argues that labour's refusal to take on constitutional reform is a major failing of its policy review, but a matter of active opposition rather than oversight. Rustin (1989: 53) suggests that labour has difficulty making democracy the centre of a radical or socialist programme. Certainly conceptions of democracy have always been used to support socialism, but it was the programme of reforms it supported, and not the processes of representation itself which labour focused on. Neither Benn and Heffer nor Charter 88 put forward a conception of democracy demanding a citizenship which defends black rights specifically.

Democracy appears in labour's policy review in relation to a field of concepts which includes citizenship and community, and which have a strategic importance to the arguments developed in this volume. What is the 'community' to which labour refers (Labour Party 1989: 6)? At one level the community referred to is obviously the nation. Communities are constructed in political discourses around specific political demands and forms of association. The demands made on behalf of the national political community are concerned with economic prosperity and modernisation. Both the identity and the political demands of the national community are maintained in the second use of the notion community in the review, the European Community.[18] 'Britain's future [the review proclaims] is in the European Community . . .' (Labour Party 1989: 7). The community within a community embraces notions of internationalism and co-operation, though in a competitive sense of securing the best deal for British workers and British pensioners. The constituencies which make up the community of the nation are workers and consumers though these are not equally valued. Most of the review is concerned with production and the importance of wealth creation; hence work emerges from the review as the most valid form of human activity, repeating an old labour theme. Work retains its old centrality in defining political concerns.

The policy review supports its two key constituencies, workers and consumers, by asserting a notion of citizenship or membership of the political community. The specification of rights is, of course, an important part of any discourse on citizenship. Worker citizenship is construed as the extension of 'democracy to the workplace' through the creation of 'flexible forms of common ownership' in which 'enterprises are owned and managed by their employees' (Labour Party 1989: 13), supported by a charter of employment rights. Labour's charter of employment rights would spell out basic entitlements to health and safety, welfare, a minimum wage, protection from discrimination, respect for family responsibilities and more flexible working arrangements.[19] These 'inalienable rights' are to be guaranteed by trade unions which, we are told, 'have a central role to play in a successful economy' (Labour Party 1989: 21). Hence an old association is maintained, recast around the centrality of the worker/citizen in the modern, wealth-creating economy. Labour's other notion of citizenship, consumer citizenship, is so broad as to be synonymous with a notion of community. 'The consumer and the community cannot be separated' (Labour Party 1988: 25) in 'supply side socialism' (Labour Party 1989: 6). This notion of consumer sovereignty was to guarantee responsiveness, in services and distribution, to the needs of the consumer. Consumers were to have more power and better protection. 'Democratic socialism is about people recognising that we depend on each other, and acting together to meet our mutual needs. That is why labour is naturally the party of the consumer' (Labour Party 1989: 41).

SOCIALISM AND RACIAL EQUALITY

The political space for the assertion of black rights is contained in labour's policy review, especially in its conception of work and consumption as forms of citizenship. A demand for social justice in consumption rights, for example, could support the demand for racial equality across a range of distribution systems concerning goods and social facilities such as health and education. Similarly notions of worker citizenship could support some important demands by black workers for equal access and opportunity. What is required are the political forces to press these demands, and labour has hindered these in its treatment of black sections. Explicitly, the inequalities suffered by black Britons receive cursory treatment in the review, which ignored the Black Agenda submitted by the Labour Party Black Sections Movement. The section of the review dealing with 'the challenge of equal opportunities' deals only with women (Labour Party 1989: 7). The review admits that black Britons need special protection by insisting that changes in the laws on discrimination are needed to provide a basis for 'equal rights as citizens of this country' (1989: 7). This is a frank admission that whilst black Britons are formally included in labour's political community as worker and consumer citizens, their formal citizenship is worthless unless their equal participation in society is underwritten by law. The review sets up black citizenship as in need of separate guarantees, and then only partially provides them[20]. Hence labour's most recent bid for social justice is fundamentally flawed in its exclusion of black rights as anything but a marginal concern.

LABOUR AS AN ENUNCIATIVE SITE IN THE 1990s

Labour, as an enunciative site in the 1990s, largely retains its 1930s structure with one or two changes which are worthy of note. The power struggle between the constituency parties, the parliamentary party and the national executive over the right to define and announce party policy remains much as it was in the 1930s. So, too, does the party's eclecticism of policy and philosophy which cuts across these key sites. But there are some important changes. Basic party policy is no longer made through the policy sub-committees of the NEC. These have been replaced by joint committees of selected national executive, parliamentary party and Trades Union Congress members. The party is still institutionally trade union dominated through the representation of trade union members on key enunciative sites like the national executive, though there are moves to rectify this. Two opposing trends are evident in current Labour Party organisation. Labour is actively applying notions of democracy to itself. It now elects its leader and deputy through an electoral college, and may yet move to a one member one vote system. Constituencies also have some power over their elected representatives in the mandatory re-selection of MPs. Selection and re-selection processes may now be more open to party members, but this has caused some bitter conflicts, and it has caused the party leadership to impose parliamentary candidates on local parties on many occasions. This imposition by the party centrally contests the trend towards democratisation. Labour is also a more centralised political machine now than at any point in its history. Although official policy is still sanctioned by conference, the national executive retains the hold it had over

41

conference in the 1930s. But there is a power-shift away from the national executive to the party leadership and the front bench of the parliamentary party, so that conference decisions can be left out of the party manifesto by the shadow cabinet, which is now powerful in defining official policy (Benn and Heffer 1986: 62). The Organisation Committee (set up in 1986 to hear and determine all disciplinary matters) rose to great prominence as labour all but abandoned policy-making in favour of attention to discipline in the mid to late 1980s. It dealt with accusation and counter-accusation in local parties about 'left' and 'right' takeovers. It dealt with expulsions and suspensions thereby taking a firmer grip on the limits of labourism than ever before in labour's history. Many local parties and local government committees were in disarray in this period.

THE LIMITS OF CONTEMPORARY LABOURISM

The 1980s defence of labourism was spearheaded by labour's register of non-affiliated groups, and recalls the black circulars of the 1930s, a practice which fell into disuse in 1973. The purpose of the register was to establish eligibility for party membership by operating clause two of the party constitution, thus excluding those members of organisations which have their own principles, structure and propaganda. All organisations wanting affiliation to the Labour Party were required to apply and be screened. Constitutional boundaries are also, of course, political boundaries, but labour was reluctant to state these (Straw 1983: 73). The focus of labour's exclusions is still the Militant Tendency whose members have described labour's attacks as 'witch hunts' (Grant 1989: xi). Actions against militant influences guided the expulsions of individual party members, as well as the expulsion of the Liverpool Labour Group by the 1986 conference (Labour Party 1986b: 13). Anxieties about Militant were also evident in placing Labour Party Young Socialists under the control of its parent party in 1982. Militant Tendency was under investigation by the Labour Party's Organisation Sub-committee from 1981 in the form of the Hayward Hughes investigation whose report was endorsed by party conference (Gordon 1982: 11–12). This distinguished organisers from members of Militant and singled the former out for expulsion, including the editorial board of

Militant newspaper, expelled in 1983. In avoiding the statement of political principles, labour objected to Militant's entryism (it was clearly unprepared to share the representation of organised labour) and not its Trotskyism. But labour was in fact defending a conception of socialism which excluded 'class struggle' between workers and employers in the industrial field, the crisis and collapse of British capitalism, and its replacement by a new political order in which workers' interests prevail (Grant 1989: 445). This effectively reasserts the same political boundaries as in the 1930s.

CONCLUSION

This chapter has shown that labourism generates a plurality of socialisms, sustained and defended by the organisational structure of the party and its disciplinarity. Whilst the limits of labourism are rarely stated explicitly, concepts like struggle, mass organisation and conflict are, and always have been, specifically excluded. The means by which socialism is purged of these concepts is through the exclusion from the party of political forces which have alternative principles of organisation. Labour sustains its conceptions of socialism through its method of sanctioning statements as official. The limits of official labourism are much more strictly defined than labourism as a whole, which sustains a range of political possibilities. The distinction between the limits of labourism and the limits of official labourism are best established in specific contexts and will be indicated in the context of the race issues dealt with in each chapter. This chapter has also shown that conceptions of socialism for the 1990s have definite historical conditions of emergence in the 1930s. The analysis of socialism in the 1990s reveals a political space, construed around a notion of citizenship rights, in which labour could seriously apply itself to race issues. Whether this, or the conception of socialism presented in the review will ever have a force in practice remains to be seen. This chapter was intended to demonstrate that whilst official labourism is construed within some strict boundaries, the boundaries of labourism as a whole allow a diversity of opportunity for struggles around human equality.

3

THE LABOUR PARTY'S COMMONWEALTH

This chapter focuses on labour's understanding of race in the 1930s in the context of political debates surrounding the demand for Indian independence. Conceptualisations of race, and its field of concepts, significantly construct labour's commonwealth at the point at which it was extended to include black citizens. This context mobilises a series of concerns which highlight black capacity for political association, and which give new meaning to the significance of the (new) commonwealth. As these debates show, constructions of Indian citizenship draw heavily on notions of racial difference and blackness acquires significances which it takes to postwar debates about new commonwealth immigration and race relations.

Labour's involvement in Indian independence may be understood at a conceptual level as attempts to construct human collectivities and their principles of association: political communities.[1] Political community is not an object of discourse, it is a principle underlying discourse, and can be any form of human collectivity constructed in discourse. Political communities have a stated common principle organising their collectivity, establishing what is common to the group. The basis for association could be geographical, religious, linguistic and so on, and may also make use of notions of racial distinctiveness. Claims to racial distinctiveness usually invoke some form of community which includes a number of forms of human association. Because this study is about political discourse and claims which have a representational dimension in labourist politics, we will refer to these communities as political communities. The debates examined in this chapter generate a number of political

44

communities – enfranchiseable Indians, Moslems, Anglo-Asians, workers, untouchables and so on. These are simply groups of human subjects constructed in a discourse on decolonisation, as having a representable basis for common association. Claims to commonality are frequently presented in terms of a set of political demands, objectives or interests. For example Indians were a political community in their demand for independence, but for the purposes of constitution-writing they were referred to as Brahmins, untouchables and so on. Commonwealth is an example of a political community, and one which has a central place in this study. Political community is used in this chapter as an analytic device to explore some of the boundaries in grouping and distinguishing human subjects.[2]

CONDITIONS OF EMERGENCE

The Indian nation, because of the way it was constructed through its independence constitution, was a political community containing other political communities. India was also a concept constructed in political discourse. This study is concerned with labour's understanding of India and the extent to which this drew upon and reconstructed notions of racial difference. Labour's India was the product of a number of constraints, which may be collectively referred to as its conditions of emergence as an object in labourist discourse. Constraints are the forces which structure an issue, which give it general direction. They may be thought of as a series of blocks which impose a general set of conditions within which only certain political possibilities and statements are possible.

The first constraint in producing India as a political issue for labour was that India had to be given independence, and progress towards this was a political expectation of the early 1930s. India had been promised independence by successive British governments.[3] As the government of India from 1929 to 1931 labour inherited this process as part of the mantle of citizenship (Mesbahuddin 1987: v, 103). Mesbahuddin (1987) has provided a detailed chronology of labour's involvement in key independence negotiations which supports the contention of this study, that labour was centrally involved in Indian independence. The issue was not should India be given independence, but when and how this should be achieved.

45

Secondly, India was the first black country to gain independence from the British empire. Prior to Indian independence in 1947 only white-ruled colonies (Canada, New Zealand, Australia, South Africa, Newfoundland and Ireland) had made the transition from empire to commonwealth. The construction of commonwealth around its old (white) and new (black) forms was about blackness, and was not the simple matter of chronology which is often presented. It was concerns about the citizenship capacities of black commonwealth subjects which delayed Indian independence and that of other black countries, thus creating the distinction between old and new commonwealth which later became important when immigration to Britain was structured by patriality.

Thirdly, the attainment of nationhood from within the British empire has always been conducted as the final act of British tutelage. The final act of the departing colonial government is its guardianship of the new political order. This has traditionally taken the form of constitutional talks in which British conceptions of good government and citizenship are reconciled with the prevailing political forces in the country demanding independence. Hence, India would not be released from the empire without constitutional talks, and it was, of course, British conceptions of citizenship which formed the standard against which black subjects were judged and found wanting.

Fourthly, India was expected to be a single nation. This requirement imposed a unity India had never possessed. Even under colonial rule, Britain had only restricted jurisdiction in the Indian states ruled by the princes.[4] In the end this constraint was challenged by the creation of Pakistan in the final settlement, when it was recognised that the divisions in India were so deep seated as to require the creation of two nations, one Hindu, the other Moslem. Hindus and Moslems were also considered, in some labour statements, to be racially distinctive populations.[5] Their racial distinctiveness was constructed around cultural, historical and religious differences.

Finally, Indian demands for independence were underscored by a campaign of civil disobedience. Indian oral history archives (held at the Nehru Memorial Library in Delhi) recording the views of national congress and trade union leaders, as well as newspaper reports in India and in Britain, indicate that British imperialism was clinging on to India by its fingernails in the late 1920s and early 1930s. Civil order had broken down to such an extent that British rule, in some areas, was only maintained by military strength.[6] The cause of Indian nationalism and its campaigns of civil disobedience were organised around a number of political forces, and these contextualise labour's involvement in Indian affairs. The most significant force contesting British colonialism in India was the Indian National Congress. This, its archives indicate, was strategically and politically diverse.[7] Other significant political forces include the Congress Socialist Party, set up to attract socialists to the nationalist cause, and the Indian Communist Party. There were also the two major factions of the Indian trade union movement, one supported (or more correctly created) by the British Labour Party, the other supported by the British Communist Party. There was the All India Socialist Party, which shared some political ground with the parts of the Indian trade union movement sponsored by the Labour Party. There were also marxist groups and the more militant Moslem factions associated with some of the acts of greater violence. Each of these political forces had its own objectives and strategies which converged in their own particular ways upon the demand for colonial freedom.

LABOUR'S INDIAN EMPIRE

Labour's commonwealth was created out of the Indian empire and is best understood in this context. The Labour government was responsible for India from 1929 to 1931, directing a brief, but significant, chapter of colonial history. Because India backed its demand for independence with a civil disobedience campaign, the labour government was faced with widespread civil unrest in India, and a growing recognition that the colonial government was being served notice to quit. Labour also presided over some significant processes in the creation of Indian nationhood: the Round Table Conferences (India Office 1930–1931, 1931a) set up to consult Indian opinion which took place in London, and two royal commissions. The Indian Statutory Commission (Home Affairs Department 1930) gave a detailed account of social conditions in India, and the Royal Commission on Labour in India (India Office 1931b), which reported on Indian working conditions, provided information used in framing the Indian constitution, and the basis for independence in 1947. The political community of nation, and its representative arrangements, were being created in India in the early 1930s under labour direction (Mesbahuddin 1987).[8] Labour's commonwealth was to include the first black nation; labour was the architect of the new commonwealth. The particular association this created between notions of racial difference and political capacity placed the couplet citizenship/race on the British political agenda, in the framework of labourist politics.

Labour's commonwealth required two things. Firstly, it required the maintenance of empire until such time as it could be properly dismantled. Secondly, in order for the empire to be dismantled it had to be understood. Labour's official involvement with the Indian empire was construed around these two principles. Opinion within the Labour Party on the political acceptability of empire varied. There were those who agreed with the Communist Party and considered that Indians had the right to overthrow the colonial government through insurrectionary struggle. There were others who considered British methods of acquiring India by 'conquest' and 'purchase' (Wise 1931: 1360) perfectly valid. There were still others who considered that a labour government was better able to secure a measure of social justice in India than any ruling Indian elite likely to take control after independence (Wedgwood 1931: 1149). But official policy considered that empire was an unacceptable political arrangement for socialists, and one which should be transformed into commonwealth, as soon as the relevant political arrangements could be set in place. Officially conceptualised as a transitional phase in the creation of an enlarged commonwealth, the empire had to be maintained. It was a condition of commonwealth. This presented the Labour Party with a serious problem. India was torn apart in the early 1930s by anti-imperialist protest. How was it to respond?

Labour maintained its Indian empire by the extensive use of armed force, and draconian policing. British rule in India was maintained by a system of ordinances which suspended civil liberties, but mostly staved off the need for military intervention. The Bombay Ordinances, for example, set up what one labour member described as the world's first concentration camps

(Heath 1934: 135) in defence of labour's empire. A letter from Nehru to Bridgeman of the League Against Imperialism[9] indicates intensive police activity in Bihar in the late 1920s, not atypical of other parts of India. 'We are having a number of police round ups and arrests all over the country. Either the police have completely lost their heads or a deliberate attempt is being made to show that vast conspiracies are afoot' (All India Congress Committee 1929–39) This is typical of accounts of its kind. It indicates the level of police activity required to maintain British sovereignty over India during the period of the labour government, and shows that labour did not shrink from maintaining the rule of (British) law.

The maintenance of public order within the empire was more than a duty, it was a political priority which displaced other priorities. This is illustrated by the case of the Meerut prisoners. The Meerut prisoners were a group of political activists and trade unionists charged with conspiracy following the organisation of industrial disruption in Calcutta and Bombay. They were trade unionists supporting the cause of anti-colonial struggle, representing what was a common association of political objectives in India at that time. Despite developing a special, if interventionist, relationship with Indian trade unions, labour was prepared to imprison trade unionists involved in nationalist agitation on the grounds that these were not proper trade union concerns. Labour chose not to release the Meerut prisoners during its period of government, but following a rising tide of protest from the British labour and trade union movement, the National Joint Council (1933a) issued an official statement offering qualified support for the prisoners. Labour's support for public order outweighed its support for organised labour, as it has done on many occasions since.

Labour's Indian empire was torn by communal conflict as well as anti-colonial protest. Communal conflict was a significant part of labour's conception of empire and a stumbling block in the construction of commonwealth. Conflict between the main religious communities was widely reported both in Britain and in India by the British-controlled news media (see, for example, *The Times* 19 June 1931: 10). Because the British government had made it clear that there was to be a federal settlement in India in which the main communities would have separate representation, this encouraged religious and other communities to press their claims for representation. Public forms of conflict reinforced these claims. This focus on conflict in understanding India served a double purpose. It cast doubt on India's capacity for self-determination, and it placed a responsibility for demonstrating statesman-like qualities on the Indian population and its political leaders. This vision of India had the official support of the Labour Party, but there were others who recognised that communal conflict was fostered by the process of constitutional settlement.

Labour's Indian empire was also socially heterogeneous. This was the premise of the Indian Statutory Commission which set out to 'discover' Indian society. The Indian Statutory Commission, which based itself on the 1921 Indian census, was a detailed investigation of India's diverse population, cross-cut by religious, cultural and socio-economic differences. This social diversity was to find expression in the constitutional arrangements for commonwealth. What kind of political arrangement could confer nationhood on so diverse a population? But this heterogeneous society was not just to be represented, it was also to be reconstructed and modernised in the processes of constitutional settlement, as the Statutory Commission and the Royal Commission on Labour in India made clear. Labour was the chief architect of this process of commonwealth-building through the modernisation of populations. For example, labour made it clear that it could not confer citizenship on a peasantry. The peasantry were to be transformed into an industrial labour force, a process considered in some detail by the Royal Commission on Labour in India.

Labour's Indian empire's most important feature was that it was in transition to the more acceptable form of commonwealth. Empire was an uneasy political formulation for labour, underpinned by human exploitation, to be gradually replaced by an enlarged commonwealth. Commonwealth could be presented as an expression of international brotherhood and co-operation, sentiments repeated in labour conference resolutions on India from the mid-1920s.

> I am a firm believer in the union of British dominions ... that together with her [India] we will start on the road to the federation of the world.... We will have to substitute

comradeship, brotherhood and co-operation, in place of
domination and imperialism . . .

(Lansbury 1931)

Official statements such as this, of international brotherhood
constructed around an argument for independence, provide a
point of tension with another strand of labour thinking. British
workers, labour's priority constituency, were privileged and
protected by the suppression of Indian industry, something
which was underwritten by imperialism and supported by labour
in its savage defence of empire in the early 1930s. Lancashire
textile operatives, for example, were kept in work because they
were protected from competition with Indian cotton workers.
This certainly problematises the spectre of an international
alliance of workers' interests. 'The great masses of the common
people in India who have the same aspirations as the masses of
the common people of Britain, will one day be united, and we
shall see both India and Britain economically free' (Buchanan
1931: 1359). If labour's two key constituencies, British workers
and Indian workers, had competing interests, how was labour to
reconcile these interests? Whose interests took priority? This
question is answered in the manner in which labour discharged
its imperial responsibilities. The interests of British workers
were paramount. An international brotherhood of workers
remains a labour proposition, yet it is always mediated by a fierce
nationalism.

Labour's Indian empire was maintained longer than it might
have been, partly because the transition to commonwealth was
mediated by other priorities which hampered the process of
transition. Labour's commitment to independence through
negotiation with Indian opinion at the Round Table Conference
ensured that constitution-building would be a tortuous process.
A slower transition was also ensured by labourist notions of
democracy. In the end these principles were sacrificed in order
to achieve an independence settlement. In the mean time labour
maintained an empire it was committed to abolishing, by the use
of armed repression. Labour's empire was not an appealing
spectre. Labour did more than inherit the Indian empire, it
significantly constructed it as a concept, and gave it political
direction at a crucial transition point in its history.

LABOUR'S COMMONWEALTH

What was labour's understanding of commonwealth and the principles upon which it was constructed? Labour's construction of commonwealth was built around a particular understanding of what constituted readiness for independence, its commitment to negotiation, its conception of democracy which demanded certain forms of representation and its belief that certain populations supported the modernisation process better than others. These dimensions making up labour's conception of commonwealth will be considered in turn.

Readiness for independence

Readiness for independence was (officially) a question of capability. Labour pledged itself to confer 'without distinction of race or colour' such measure of self-determination as 'they [subject populations] are capable of exercising' (New Fabian Research Bureau 1928: 4). The capacity for citizenship was unequally (and racially) distributed as the Labour Party's (1933c) major statement on colonial policy, 'The Colonies', makes clear. This conceptualised a hierarchy of capability, indexed in forms of culture and the extent to which these were recognisably European. For example, some dependencies (labour cites Mediterranean countries, the Falkland Islands and the West Indies) are described as 'European in culture, language, religion and industry. No question arises of "natives" '. Then there were dependencies of an 'oriental culture' which were in the process of industrialising. Finally there were 'dependencies inhabited mainly by peoples of a primitive culture' (the African and Pacific countries) where independence was a distant prospect (Labour Party 1933c: 17). Labour's construction of commonwealth organised a field of concepts which included culture, industrialisation and so on as significant in distinguishing degrees of readiness for citizenship. These were ways of classifying human populations which also had other ways of being identified, using notions of race. 'The Colonies' refers to 'British and other European races' distinguished from 'native communities' (Labour Party 1933c: 3). The discursive association between race, culture, industry and citizenship capacity was certainly not new. But labour sustained this conceptual clustering, and used it to generate a notion of commonwealth just as the black empire was poised to join.

There is, however, no hint in 'The Colonies' that even the most 'primitive' of 'native'[s] was forever beyond citizenship. Independence, and the citizenship it required, were processes mediated by education and not backed by membership of racial categories:

> Obstacles existing in many parts of the empire, of multitudinous languages, of ignorance of industrial technique, of inexperience of free association, must be overcome by deliberate and detailed educational schemes designed to assist even the most primitive type of Native to become a free citizen capable of efficient participation and control of his industry and government.
>
> (Labour Party 1933c: 13)

Racial categorisations were used to differentiate stages in readiness for citizenship, but not to determine these stages. Potentially, all British colonies could become dominions. But a process of modernisation was required to achieve this.

Commonwealth citizenship

Negotiation with Indian opinion was the second principle around which labour's commonwealth was construed. The processes this involved were instrumental in constructing notions of commonwealth citizenship. The Round Table Conferences were to provide just this opportunity. They were a labour initiative and instrumental in settling the structure of the constitution on which independence was eventually based (Mesbahuddin 1987: vii). Their significance was that they provided, in their delegate structure, a list of the representable populations in labour's India.[10] Moslems, Anglo-Indians, workers, Indian commerce, Hindus, the Indian National Congress (Gandhi-supporting faction and not more radical elements), women, European commerce, landlords, the army and the princes who ruled in the Indian states made up the voice of India at the Round Table Conferences. Here it becomes evident that labour's notion of citizenship, as the collective capacity of a political community, is actually a matter of the capacities attributed to groups making up the political community. Labour's category 'India' does not refer to its population as a whole. Some groups are more important than others in construing nations.

Peasants, who formed the bulk of the Indian population, were a major population category deemed unrepresentable and hence excluded from the Round Table. Labour's numerous statements of the time, establishing solidarity with the masses of India, of course also included peasants who were, in practice, difficult to distinguish from the workers to whom labour was explicitly committed.[11] The peasant 'with an outlook confined by tradition and environment' was considered incapable of anything bigger than local, village, political processes (Home Affairs Department 1930: 19). The acquisition of citizenship was thought to be constrained by material culture. Through a use of agricultural metaphor, the peasant's mind, as well as the peasant's material culture, was seen as rooted in the soil and traditions of ages. It was precisely this rooting of mind and mode of subsistence which posed peasants as objects of social reform rather than as citizens. If peasants were to be included in any notion of citizenship, it would be through their transformation into an industrial labour force. A modern political order, based on citizenship, required the eradication of the peasantry. Labour's official conception of India as a member of the commonwealth, derived from the Statutory Commission, excluded the majority of its (black) population.

Untouchables provide another example of a population in need of modernisation, for although they were represented at the Round Table, their spokesperson was not an untouchable. Untouchables were also represented in the 1935 constitution, but only in a token sense. They were referred to at the conferences by their representative as 'serfs' and 'slaves' (Ambedkar 1930–1: 131). They were presented as the remnants of a feudal order, incapable of supporting a notion of nationhood or citizenship. The only hope of untouchables achieving a political voice was through their transformation into workers. Worker, for labour, was a category which was to act as a collection point in forging citizenship for populations whose traditional mode of existence placed them beyond citizenship. The issue of untouchability, like the issue of the peasantry, tied the modernisation of India and the construction of citizenship together. Modernisation was a key concept used to construe labour's commonwealth. It served to distinguish populations as well as social and economic processes.

There were populations which could support modernisation, and populations which could not. The extent to which a population was involved in processes which supported modernisation, was taken as an indicator of its capacity for citizenship. It is to the link between citizenship and modernisation that we now turn.

Some examples of modernising populations demonstrating citizenship potential include Anglo-Indians, Indian commerce and, of course, workers. An examination of what precisely these populations offered the development process allows a closer examination of what was at stake in the term citizenship.

Anglo-Indians were considered a distinctive part of Indian nationhood by virtue of their contribution to Indian society. They had, in the view of the Statutory Commission (Home Affairs Department 1930: 44–5), contributed to the development of India by supporting the forces of law and order under colonial rule, serving in minor administrative posts in the Indian civil service as well as in the police and army. This was seen as evidence of their capacity for citizenship of a modern political order. Anglo-Indians were further distinguished in rather precise parentage terms, drawn from a discourse on genetics, in an appendix to the Statutory Commission's report. As Anglo-Indians themselves expressed it at the Round Table Conference 'We represent in our very bodies that fusion of East and West' (Gidney 1930–1: 74). This claim to racial distinctiveness under-pinned claims that they were a force for modernisation. They were a remnant, not of a feudal order like the peasantry, but an altogether more developed order deposited by British imperialism. Even though labour did not generate these statements it adopted their rationale by including Anglo-Indians in the constitutional negotiations and the eventual settlement. In so doing it aided the association of citizenship with the forces of law and order.

Indian commerce's claim to be a constituent part of the Indian nation was considered by the Statutory Commission to be backed by its contribution to industrialisation and modernisation in India. Industrialisation surfaces again as the basis of a modern political system. 'Commerce and industry are the life blood of the nation. Political freedom is not going to mean anything to us unless we have economic freedom ...' (Mody 1930–1;155–6). The ability of Indian commerce to establish the economic basis for political freedom and challenge the domination of European interests constituted its claim to citizenship. Labour's commitment to industrialisation as a force underpinning citizenship serves to reinforce the point that labour was committed to eradicating the conditions which sustained the peasantry. The industrialisation of India was thus central in the construction of citizenship.

Indian workers, revealed by the Royal Commission to live in the most miserable conditions of abject poverty, could not possibly live up to the citizenship potential of the commercial classes or Anglo-Indians. But as labour's priority constituency they had to be given some form of representation. Labour's conceptualisation of workers as citizens stressed their potential for education towards citizenship. The development of workers towards citizenship was a process which could, appropriately, occur through unionisation. Labour calculated this to have two effects. Firstly, it would establish proper, bona fide, trade unions in India which could struggle for improvements in working conditions (itself a modernising influence on industry); and secondly, workers could be enfranchised by giving trade unions reserved seats in federal and provincial assemblies hence giving them a limited form of citizenship. Participation in trade unions was seen as an education for citizenship because it involved participation in political processes. 'The proper representation of labour is itself educative; the recognition of its claims as part of the body politic will bring increased responsibility and a sense of unity within the community as a whole' (India Office 1931b: 462). Under labour direction the Royal Commission established an understanding of the link between trade unionism and citizenship. Its central concerns were distinguishing legitimate from unacceptable trade unionism, and the contribution to citizenship of the proper practices of trade unionism. 'Trade Unionism, to be fully effective, demands two things: a democratic spirit and education. The democratic ideal has still to be developed in the Indian worker, and the lack of education is the most serious obstacle of all' (India Office 1931b: 321). Labour took the opportunity presented by the need to construct Indian citizenship, to define legitimacy in trade unionism (based on British forms) and defend it from the Communist Party.

In order to establish the proper principles of trade unionism and mobilise it in the education of Indian workers for citizenship, labour had to reconstruct the Indian trade union movement. This bid to establish the principles of British social democracy in place of British imperialism took place around independence negotiations. Labour created the Indian Trades Union Federation (in 1929) in order to represent Indian workers at the Round Table Conference. It did so because the existing body, the All India Trades Union Congress, refused to take part in constitutional negotiations, and demonstrated what for labour was an unacceptable commitment to anti-imperialist struggle. As one Indian trade union leader expressed it: 'Trades unions are just good weapons to fight the British' (Banergee 1977). Although labour supported colonial freedom, this blurred the distinction between legitimate industrial struggles (which were properly the concern of trade unions) and nationalist political agitation (which was not). The Trades Union Federation was set up in the image of the British Trades Union Congress (Trades Union Federation 1929). Correspondence between the TUC and the Trades Union Federation shows that the British trade union movement saw itself as model and educator (Trades Union Federation 1929–32). Labour's conception of proper trade unions was established against the ad hoc strike committees organised by the Indian Communist Party, which had been successful in creating industrial havoc in the 1920s. Proper trade unions had an organisational structure, democratically elected representatives, were economical in their use of the strike weapon and resistant to general strikes. Above all, proper trade unions were opposed to acts of violence and public disorder, and the broader political objectives of nationalism set out by the Royal Commission (India Office 1931b: 325). Labour's conception of social democracy and trade unionism, through which it construed workers as members of the Indian political community, may be seen as the distinctly socialist contribution to commonwealth-building. This, like the imperialism it replaced, denied Indian autonomy and political capacity.

Democracy and commonwealth

The third principle around which labour's commonwealth was constructed concerns standards of democracy. Official labourist conceptions of democracy in the context of domestic socialism stress the classic formulations of Mill (see Durbin 1935: 379) in prioritising the expression of the general will of a people through parliamentary processes. The capacity for this was not universal, but a matter of the state of mind of a people, and a property of those higher up the political evolutionary scale (Durbin 1940: 151). Labour's limited conception of the representable political community in India supports the view that Indians lacked the level of mental evolution required by democratic process. Labour's construction of democracy in India also occurred around principles quite different from those which established the British political community. It was not entirely clear what democracy might mean in India. The debate about this in the Labour Party was how the principles of democracy could best serve the politics of socialism, in protecting the disadvantaged, and how this could be reconciled with Indian demands for political freedom (Wedgwood 1931: 1143–5). In the end labour neither protected the disadvantaged nor constructed a model of government in India which offered a proper democracy. India was, eventually, awarded a peculiar form of federation which failed to enfranchise most of its population. Labour was instrumental in awarding India a unique form of second class citizenship.

Black commonwealth citizenship was constructed around a particular form of federation and franchise. Federation was regarded as the political arrangement suited to India's social diversity. It had a certain status as the model used in other, white-ruled dominions, notably Canada. 'Canadian model for India' ran a *Times of India* headline (1931: 1). Its benefits as a system of political representation were explored philosophically by Jefferson, who found it to be closer to the 'principles of human nature' (Padover 1943: 124) than other forms of government. But there were some important differences between the use of the federal system in North America and in India. The North American model of federation was territorial, and not the combination of territorial divisions and a communally divided electorate which was eventually implemented in India. The Indian federation selectively incorporated into the political community of nation the representable populations by giving them seats on the provincial assemblies in proportion to their numbers in any given area. Under these arrangements provincial assemblies were not expressions of the political will of an area (as in Mill) but a plurality of competing wills. In Mill's terms India was a plurality of nations and not a single people or political community sharing 'common sympathies' or a 'feeling' of nationhood generated by a 'community of recollections' (Mill 1968: 306). The type of federation set up in India meant that Provincial Assemblies contained collections of political communities, workers, commerce and so on, each with its own basis for commonality. These political communities were based on a medley of distinctions such as gender, economic interests, religious affiliations and so on, and not on their association with a geographically defined area sanctioned by Jefferson. Hence these were political communities constructed around restricted expressions of political interest, as opposed to a community of recollections. Workers, for example, were not only poorly represented, their citizenship was restricted to the expression of their interests as workers. They were not citizens, articulating the general will in their geographical area, they were worker-citizens. Their forms of political participation were thus functional and restricted by a limited form of trade unionism. Labour constructed in India a federation which could support only a restricted conception of citizenship.

The federal structure proposed for India in the early 1930s remained more or less in place until 1952. It was partially implemented by the Government of India Act (1935) which divided India into a provincial and a federal structure, each with its own area of responsibility, and with federal affairs remaining in British hands until full independence in 1947. A full discussion of the constitutional details of this is provided by Mesbahuddin (1987: 168–73). The one important exception to the arrangements of the 1930s concerns the creation of Pakistan. Under intense pressure from the Moslem league, India divided into two.

The British (labour) designed federation remained until 1952 when elections were held on the basis of full adult suffrage. Labourist notions of democracy, developed to serve the cause of socialism in Britain, demanded a universal adult franchise. Mill's classic notion of a political community required, for each individual, a voice in a representative democracy. 'Any proportion of mankind are better adapted in proportion to their degree of general improvement. As they range lower and lower in development, that form of government will be, generally speaking less suitable to them' (Mill 1968: 218). No attempt was made by labour to insist on this principle in relation to Indians, who were, by implication, at the lower end of the scale of political development. Under the arrangements for provincial autonomy implemented by the Government of India Act (1935) the 50 per cent of the seats in provincial assemblies not awarded on the basis of a property qualification were allocated on a communal basis with communities being represented in the following proportions:[12] Untouchables (3 per cent); backward classes and tribes (1 per cent); Sikhs (2 per cent); Moslems (30 per cent); Anglo-Indians (0.7 per cent); Europeans (2 per cent); Indian Christians (1 per cent); commerce (3 per cent); labour (2 per cent); landlords (1 per cent); universities (0.5 per cent); and women (3 per cent). This was labour's political community in India. The only group to receive sizeable representation, besides the propertied, were Moslems. Peasants were virtually excluded and women and workers were poorly represented, though the demographic data necessary to substantiate this point is not available. In 1947 India was awarded independence on the basis of a constitution which probably only enfranchised 14 per cent of its population.[13] Labour secured, through federation and franchise, a citizenship for Indians which announced their limitations in political association.

Race and commonwealth

The association between citizenship capacity and racial difference was common currency in the 1930s in labour, and other, political discourses. Labour brought these two concepts into a discourse which established a limited form of citizenship for black commonwealth citizens. The notion of racial difference had a complex relationship to the Indian population. It was used to sustain arguments asserting Indian unity, as well as arguments asserting Indian diversity. Indian racial unity surfaced around claims that Indians were a 'cultured race', or a 'civilised race' (Lansbury 1931: 1397). Alternatively, Indian racial unity arose from the 'historical disability of being incapable of ruling' and hence 'fated to be ruled by some sort of outside race' (Wise 1931: 1360). Each of these constructions of Indian racial unity is addressing independence. Race is used to support and contest Indian political freedom. It is a multi-purpose concept.

Indians were also understood in terms of racial plurality. That this attracted official labour support is evident in the manner in which the Indian situation was finally settled. The Indian Statutory Commission (Home Affairs Department 1930: 24), for example, distinguished 'The learned and subtle Brahmin of Benares' from the '"untouchables" of Dravidian stock'. The distinction between Brahmins and Dravidians is a distinction constructed in comparative philology, to which we will return. The statutory commission, as well as identifying racially distinct parts of the Hindu fold, distinguished Hindus from Moslems also using a notion of race. In explaining that Moslem/Hindu relations were not just about religious differences, the Indian Statutory Commission (Home Affairs Department 1930: 25) comments: 'Differences of race, a different system of law and the absence of intermarriage constitute a far more effective barrier.' Similar distinctions, made around concepts like (different levels of) civilisation, culture, different juridical systems and linguistic distinctiveness as well as racial classifications, were articulated by Indian delegates themselves at the Round Table Conference.

It is evident, from the use of notions of racial difference to construe both the unity and diversity of Indians, that race is a device used to construct political communities, and that political communities can be construed around any principle at all. In this case the principle is capacity for citizenship. This makes the point that racial classifications are political constructs employed for specific purposes. Indians can be a single race, or they can be a plurality of different races. This is not an arbitrary set of distinctions, but depends on the reasons why racial categories are being construed. Race, therefore, is used to organise a range of human distinctions construed in discourse. It invokes human collectivities for specific purposes. It is also evident that race is a concept which relies on other concepts in the task of constructing political communities, and is given a meaning through the uses to which it is put. The Indian Statutory Commission statement, cited above, refers to differences in law, custom, civilisation, culture and language. These concepts are also used to construe levels of human distinction, and are reinforced by notions of racial difference. Race gives these concepts an added force

61

because it alludes to a fixity in the domain of natural, rather than social, processes. The debate concerning Indian independence yielded a field of concepts, notably order, industry, progress and so on, which distinguished the more developed parts of the Indian population from the rest. These are also distinctions used in establishing notions of racial difference. It is by now apparent that the race concept activated a field of concepts in its use in the context of Indian independence, and that these concerned distinctions in human capacity and especially citizenship.

The construction of racial distinctions around notions of human capacity was not just a feature of these debates, but a long established association employed for new purposes. The race concept in these debates drew upon notions of citizenship capacity, because this was what the debate was about – were Indians capable of self-government? This points to a further feature of the race concept. Race is used to construe political communities around a set of political demands, and this explains why Indians were both racially homogenous and racially diverse. Claims to Indian racial unity were, in fact, made around two divergent political projects. The use of race in this context supports both an attempt collectively to dismiss Indians as in- capable of citizenship, and an attempt to include them all in a collectivity of capability. Lansbury's (1931) assertion of Indian racial unity was, in fact, an attempt to secure a universal franchise, and was one of the main tension points with official labour policy. The point that race is a device used to construct political communities around specific political demands, is also supported by claims asserting that India was a racially plural society.

What is at stake in the use of race to establish notions of human capacity? Notions of an 'Indian mind' (MacDonald 1931: 1102), which could be translated into a constitution, were implicit in labour pronouncements about the state of readiness of Indians for independence. India both contained a single mind, and a collection of minds, at different stages of readiness for citizenship. Much of the debate in labour circles concerning the fitness of Indians for independence focused on their 'state of mind' (Attlee 1931: 1120), as though Indians possessed a collective mental capacity which could be read from an investigation of their society. Mental capacity is a familiar theme in discourses concerning racial differences. A link between states of mind and political capacities was well established by the social contract theorists, who speak of the outlook of a political community and its relationship to the ability to sustain the practice of political association. Mill's classic work on liberty (1968), for example, makes reference to the capacity for order and progress as a set of mental characteristics, attributable to a people. Racial classifications, which took account of mind and citizenship capacity, were not invented by the Labour Party. But the Labour Party applied them in constructing a commonwealth which included black subjects, and so gave force to concerns that the capacity for political community was lacking in black commonwealth populations. This is supported by references in 'The Colonies' (Labour Party 1933c: 16) to black peoples constituting a 'subject' population, and by references in parliament to the treatment of India being linked to 'colour' (Jones 1931: 1326). This association between citizenship and colour was not inevitable, it was constructed. Even conceptions of racial difference did not necessarily require the attribution of a significance to skin colour. There were other systems of racial classification available to labour in the 1930s.

The link between state of mind and skin colour was established in the late eighteenth century in the work of Cuvier and others in comparative anatomy and craniometry (Stocking 1969: 35–41). Notions of the relationship between material culture and a state of development are familiar in, for example, the anthropological work of E.B. Tylor in the 1870s (Stocking 1969: 72–3). The idea that material artifacts index a state of mental development goes back at least to the nineteenth century. It is evident that labour drew upon these different notions of racial classification, and used them to insist on both the unity and diversity of Indians. The primary significance of skin in the construction of racial classifications is challenged by accounts of race which attribute a primacy to other forms of distinction, for example, language. Philological (linguistic) notions of race were also employed in labour discourse. The notion of linguistic race grouped Sanskrit, Persian, Greek, Italian, Slavic, Lithuanian, Armenian and Celtic languages and led to the adjective 'Indo-European' being used to link certain Indian and European languages (Leopold 1974: 587). The notion of linguistic race was given a social context around 1850 through the reconstruction of Indo-European myths and cultural similarities, and at the same time the term Aryan (spelt Arian) supplanted Indo-European. Leopold argues that between 1850 and 1870 language became accepted as a form of human classification, seen in the work of James Cowles Pritchard in the 1840s. The logic of philological classifications of peoples was that (some) Indians of the higher castes belonged to the same racial category as Europeans, with a heritage in an ancient civilisation (as Lansbury suggested) and its political arrangements. Henry Maine suggests that Aryans established self-governing village councils in India and Europe. The oldest and purest remains of this culture he considered to be preserved in India (Leopold 1974: 582). By this argument Aryan culture and, by extension, the Aryan race was both distinctive from, and superior to, others. For Maine, Indians were 'of the very family of mankind to which we belong' (Leopold 1974: 582). This understanding of racial difference does not place the citizenship capacities of India in question.

The discussion of racial classification constructed around languages makes the point that skin, and other physical attributes, are only significant if they are construed in discourse as significant. Skin has no intrinsic significance; it is attributed a significance in discourse. Labour had linguistic conceptions of race, conferring racial equality with Europeans on at least some Indians, available to it in its dealings with Indian citizenship. It chose instead to attribute a significance to black skin as a sign of membership of racial categories.

CONCLUSION

Labour's commonwealth was structured by notions of socialism developed to deal with domestic politics, especially notions of public order and democracy. Labour's official commitment to these principles guided its administration of the empire and its transition to commonwealth. Labour was active in creating India as a dominion in terms which guaranteed India's status as a second class nation. In doing this it placed the notion of political capacity within a racial context which attributed a particular significance to black skin. It has been possible to trace, through the debates about Indian independence, the ways in which race was used as a device to construct political communities around political demands. The race concept emerged from labour's dealings with Indian independence as an assembly of physical characteristics, and the capacity for political association. Skin and mind were attributed a particular significance by the Labour Party in a debate about citizenship which placed in question the capacity of black commonwealth citizens for political association. The new (black) commonwealth acquired a status through Indian independence which was to become significant in organising responses to black immigration to Britain in the 1950s.

4

ANTI-SEMITISM IN
EAST LONDON

This case study of anti-semitism in East London reveals aspects of labour's conceptualisation of race which were not evident in the case study on Indian independence. It concerns conceptualisations of race applied to Britain, which forced labour to consider the issue of the multi-racial political community and the process by which it was established: immigration. Anti-semitism forced labour to consider Jewishness, and that against which Jewishness was defined, Englishness. A particular kind of Englishness was at stake here, constructed with reference to East London. Jewishness and East End Englishness are concepts which construe political communities. We are interested in how these concepts were constructed, their field of concepts, and uses made of notions of racial difference. Notions of racial difference in this case study do not draw upon skin colour as a discursive object, but employ other notions of physical distinctiveness.

This chapter will argue that labour's official responses to anti-semitism were contextualised by a commitment to judicial processes, a repudiation of public disorder, and a concern to represent particular political constituencies. These early labour approaches to race issues in Britain thus occurred within a highly restricted framework of socialism (explored in chapter two). This chapter will show that labour's constructions of Jewishness included some distinctive notions of social pathology. Race emerges from its encounter with anti-semitism with a particular constellation of concepts linking notions of an alien status with negative social attributes. This made it difficult for labour to conceptualise a political community containing more than one racially defined population.

66

Multi-racialism acquired a problematic status in these discourses which it retained into the 1960s.

EAST LONDON AND LABOUR

East London was a concept as much as a place. It was a political community construed in labourist discourse around a range of problems and constituencies with which labour associated itself, and the cause of socialism. East London's poor, working class population had been the object of philanthropic scrutiny through the Oxford and Cambridge missions in the nineteenth century which brought the privileged into contact with the dispossessed. East London contained labour's priority constituencies, and was a forcing house for social reform. Social reform was one of labour's principle objectives, and pivotal in defining socialism. The East End was, and still is, a poor inner city area, historically associated with immigration. Hugenot refugees had moved there in the seventeenth century, the Irish in the mid-nineteenth century, and Jewish refugees driven out of Eastern Europe by the pogroms followed. This brought Jewish immigration to Britain to a peak between 1870 and 1914 (Gartner 1973: 15, Garrard 1971: 3, Fishman 1975: 3–30). East London, like poorer parts of other large cities, had a sizeable Jewish population. It was also, historically, the centre of anti-semitic agitation. The British Brothers' League, formed in 1902, operated there under the slogan 'England for the English' (Nugent and King 1979: 32). The League was later replaced by Oswald Mosley's British Union of Fascists, set up in 1932 following the collapse of the New Party, which Mosley had left the Labour Party to establish.[1] The East End of London also had historic associations with insurrectionary working class activity, of which the bread riots were an example (Jones 1976: 343). All of these factors which constitute the distinctiveness of East London, construct it as a concept in labour discourse.

The involvement of the Labour Party in the lives of local East End people replaced liberalism after the first world war, and the culture of poverty became steeped in labour and trade union practices. Poplarism, a form of municipal socialism, implemented a minimum wage in the old East London borough of Poplar in the 1920s, to the annoyance of the Transport and

67

General Workers' Union. Labour was part of the social fabric of East London. Labour's political heritage in liberal social welfare reforms and Fabianism is evident in the ways in which the party operated in East London. Both of labour's key constituencies, workers and the poor, were heavily represented in this area. By the 1930s local politics in East London were run by the Labour Party, which often acted as the advocate of local people in a material as well as a spiritual sense. The absorption by labourism of social welfare was evident in the cards distributed around the borough by the mayor of Bethnal Green, bearing the message: 'When you want advice on any matter, housing, pensions, compensation etc, come to the Labour Party office' (North East Bethnal Green Labour Party 1934). Prominent labour politicians, such as Lansbury, were active around both social welfare issues and the methodist church which was involved in organising social activities in the borough, linking the causes of socialism and methodism[2] (Lansbury 1935, 1929–35, Benningfield 1977). Labour's involvement in East London involved church social activities, social welfare case work, strong trade union organisation (especially around the docks) and responding to the political challenge of the British Union of Fascists. It was around labour's dealings with the anti-semitic campaign of the British Union (examined in greater detail in chapter seven), that labour's conceptions of Jewishness in the 1930s, the subject of this chapter, surfaced.

JEWISHNESS

What did Jewishness mean to Labour? One way of answering this question is to see how Jewishness[3] fitted into labour's vision of East London. One of the principal tensions in labourist discourses focusing on anti-semitism concerns the extent to which Jews were presented as an integral part of the political community of East London, or as a distinctive enclave within that community. Jews could never be completely indistinguishable from the political community of East London, or the term Jew would cease to have any meaning. It only has meaning in relationship to an otherness, or non-Jewishness, described as Englishness[4] (Roberts 7 November 1936: 698). Jews were conceptualised by some in the Labour Party as a part of the East

London working class and exploited masses: a conceptualisation shared with the Communist Party (Heath 1934: 135). This was also Lansbury's analysis and one which incorporated Jewish people into labour's East End constituency of the poor and working class. This, of course, dissected Jewishness as a constituency, excluding wealthy Jews, towards whom socialists have a history of antagonism (Garrard 1971: 189–202). The incorporation of Jewishness into the working class led to a hierarchy of social differences in which racial distinctions were subsidiary to what were considered to be more substantial, economic divisions such as class. This did not deny racial categorisations, but placed them in a class context. Other assessments of Jews conferred on them a distinctiveness as guests. 'What right has one section of the community to point the finger to a section to which we have given hospitality for centuries?' (Inskip 15 October 1936: 2). This assertion of the distinctiveness of Jews, which required their conceptualisation as a racially distinct category not appropriately dealt with by class politics, was quite close to the official labour position. This, of course, recognised that Jews had a parallel structure to labourism in separate trade unions, the Jewish Labour Party (the Poale Zion) and the Jewish National Labour Council. Recognition of the distinctive structures of Jewish labourism meant that labour was not claiming Jews as a labour constituency, a point which was in conflict with the politics advocated by Lansbury and the Communist Party (Knowles 1979: 52–5). Labourism had an ambivalent relationship to Jewishness as a constituency construed in political discourse. This has important implications in locating Jews as a political community.

The claim that Jews were racially distinct was important in establishing their separateness as a political community. Notions of racial difference helped establish Jewishness and Englishness as references to distinctive political communities. In a statement which was fairly typical of its time, an article in the *New Statesman and Nation*[5] attributes political disturbances in East London to the 'fact that its population is made up of members of two very different [English and Jewish] races' (Roberts 7 November 1936: 698). This reflects official labour thinking, as Jews were referred to as a race in labour's government paper 'Statement on Palestine' (Labour Party 1930b: 4) and by Herbert Morrison

(1936: 115–16). So far we have established that Jewishness was constructed as a political community with a specified relationship to other political communities and it utilised notions of racial distinctiveness. In order to further this understanding we need to know something about the field of concepts construed around Jewishness in discourse.

Jewishness was constructed as a racial category by drawing upon anatomy. References to facial features were prominent in pinpointing Jewishness. But so too were other objects of discourse including the view that Jews had a 'different glandular and emotional make-up' from the average Englishman (Roberts 1936: 698). Here, the physical features of Englishness, which remain undescribed, form the yardstick against which Jewishness is measured and made visible. Glands ambiguously substitute for skin as objects of discourse. Jewishness was also construed with reference to cultural differences from the host population. British Jews kept a religious distinctiveness in Judaeism, which imposed its own requirements in terms of the sabbath, religious festivals, family forms and food. Jews had their own languages and modes of dress which rendered them visible, and distinctive from the rest of East London, which implicitly assumed a cultural homogeneity in discourse. Jewishness also assumed an institutional distinctiveness in employment in the garment sweat shops, separate charitable and friendly societies, trade unions, Labour Party, (the Poale Zion)[6] and the Board of Deputies of Anglo Jewry which pronounced primarily on religious matters and asserted the unity of all Jews around the practices of Judaeism.

Jewishness in labour discourse was also constructed in terms of (un-English) forms of behaviour. A distinctive 'code of social conduct' made Jews 'pushful' and 'persistently industrious' (Roberts 1936: 698). Industriousness was a positive quality in the context of developing, in Indian workers, the proper habits of industrial and political participation. But in this context it was an over-assertiveness, a threat, to the lesser industriousness of Englishness represented by East London workers. This supports the idea of Jews as an invading force, threatening the jobs and homes of East Londoners, thrusting wedges of un-Englishness into the heart of an English city and thus claiming it. Mile End, for example, became 'progressively occupied by Jews until almost every house in the street, including every little corner shop, has come to be in Jewish occupation' (Roberts 1936: 698). Fears of sweating, linked to competition between East End workers and the Jewish garment shops were prominently voiced by labour. Sweating implies an illicit form of labour, an over-industriousness and a threat to other, English jobs which had won higher wages through the protection of trade unionism. Concerns like this, which comment on competition between populations over scarce resources, invoke notions of unequal right to social resources, in which Englishness has a prior claim. The construction of Jewishness as a racial category occurred through a field of concepts concerned with invasion and competition, which resurfaced in response to black immigration to postwar Britain.

Jewishness was also constructed through the concept immigrant. Jews were the objects of Britain's first systematic piece of immigration control legislation, the Aliens Act of 1905 (Solomos 1989: 34) designed to exclude aliens in penury, thus cementing the association between poverty and immigration. This extended previous forms of exclusion designed to restrict the diseased and political agitators, and conferred upon Jews a particular status in British political discourse. Jews were aliens whose claims to access to, and subsequent membership of the political community, must be scrutinised. The labour movement was divided over the control of aliens. The Trades Union Congress conference passed resolutions calling for immigration control to protect the jobs of English trade unionists from Jewish incursion in 1892, 1894 and 1895, though there was also a considerable pro-alien lobby (Garrard 1971: 174–5). These are the origins of labour's ambivalence towards immigration controls, which consisted of a form of protectionism towards British jobs and toward the social fabric of the inner city. Alien restriction, of course, made immigration to Britain by Jews fleeing the concentration camps in the 1930s (especially in the context of the protectionism engendered by high unemployment) especially difficult.[7] Most of the Jews living in East London by the 1930s were not immigrants, yet they were construed as a category in political discourse through references to an exterior set of origins.

Jewishness was also constructed in labourist discourse as an object of social reform. Numerous statements at the time comment on the conditions of poverty and exploitation in which Jews lived and worked, and are reminiscent of concerns about Indian workers. Although the entire population of East London was, historically, an object of social reform, Jews were conceptualised as a disadvantaged enclave within a more generally disadvantaged population. Hence, Jewish membership of the dispossessed was staked out in material terms, but significantly, this was also mediated by forms of racial distinction. Poverty, race and the need for social reform were a significant conceptual clustering to emerge from these discourses.

Jewishness was also the object and victim of racially motivated attacks (Joint Consultative Committee of the London Trades Council and the London Labour Party 1934). British Union of Fascists' slogans in East London, and other large cities, invoked racial imagery, notions of racial superiority, and associated Jews with international finance and communism. In addition to verbal abuse, Jews were the victims of physical attacks on their persons and property. There is evidence that the incidence of reported attacks on Jews was high, and that some of these had resulted in death. This was coupled with criticism of ineffective policing, prompting a trend towards Jewish self-defence.[8] Linked to this was the construction of Jewishness as a focus for political agitation. This, rather than a distaste for racial persecution, or an attempt to improve Jewish living and working conditions, was labour's major political focus (see chapter seven). The British Union of Fascists was responsible for organising much of the anti-semitic activity in East London which was quite intense from 1934 to 1937 (*New Statesman and Nation* 10 October 1936: 496–7). This was met by opposition from anti-fascists, opposing fascist rallies and marches through Jewish areas, provoking street disturbances. This association between Jewishness and disorder added to the contextualisation of Jews as a threat to the social fabric. Officially, labour's distaste for public disorder outweighed its distaste for anti-semitic attack, as chapter seven demonstrates in discussing labour's approach to anti-racism.

Jewishness emerged as a racial category from labourist discourse constructed with the aid of a field of concepts which established a catalogue of social pathologies. Jews were a physically, culturally and institutionally distinctive political community. They were an alien, invading population whose access to Britain was controlled by immigration legislation. Jews were also an object of social reform, victims of racial attacks and a force for violence and public disorder. The inner city has become a metaphor for many of these social problems, used to construe racial categorisation. The political community against which Jewishness was constructed, Englishness, had only a shadowy existence in the debates concerning anti-semitism. This is because Englishness is not defined, it is being defended. It is being defended from Jewishness, and this is apparent in the clustering of concepts through which Jewishness was constructed. Jewishness was a racial category constructed for the purpose of defending Englishness. That racial categorisations are used in constructing political communities around specific purposes, was noted in chapter three. Englishness was the opposite of Jewishness, and is defended around the establishment of a prior claim to jobs, proper social conditions and better resources. Englishness is constructed around an appeal to order and prosperity and an unchallenged right of access to Britain.

MULTI-RACIALISM

The term multi-racial is used to refer to a discursive political community containing more than one population defined with reference to notions of racial difference. It was not a term of the discourse in this period, but was used much later. In fact the political community of East London was a bi-racial community in labourist discourse, and a site of antagonism, competition and social disorder, as of course is evident from labour's construction of Jewishness and Englishness as oppositional categories. Neither Jewishness nor bi-racialism need have been constructed in these terms, nor given these particular political significances. There were accounts of human brotherhood, and the cohesiveness of the East London political community, offered in the kind of labourism articulated by Lansbury. The fact that labour constructed multi-racialism in these terms is revealing of official labourist approaches to race issues, and the social and political value attached to Jewishness. Labour's uneasiness about multi-racialism surfaces again in the 1950s, but as far as the 1930s were concerned, the disorder and conflict inherent in multi-racialism were clearly an affront to labourism. Accordingly, multi-racial Britain could only be a temporary arrangement.

Two possibilities concerning the disposal of the multi-racial community were presented, both of which found their way into official labour statements. The first was assimilation. Jews could assimilate to the point where they were no longer visible as a distinctive community, but an indistinguishable part of the political community of East London. The assimilation of Jews into Englishness was commented upon by prominent labour members, who recognised that there were many Jewish people within their own ranks who had abandoned Judaeism and its associated practices and behaviours, or relegated it to the private domain. In this context, economic and political distinctions would become more significant than racial demarcations, and Jews would become members of the East London working class and a labour constituency. Assimilation would require Jews to abandon their visibility, their distinctiveness and the public practice of their religion. This is what assimilation meant in official labour discourse at this time. It has since had other meanings, for this melting into Englishness was never an option for those whose racial distinctiveness was indexed in skin colour.

The second possibility which, like the first, renders the multi-racial community a temporary arrangement, concerns the removal of British Jews to Palestine.[9] Labour's commitment to the Zionist cause, the belief that Palestine was the historic homeland of the Jews, was established in labour discourse around biblical authority, and in arguments which considered Jews to have earned the right to a refuge from religious persecution. Calls for a Jewish homeland were certainly incorporated into labour conference resolutions. 'The Labour Party is the only party which has repeatedly declared at its Annual Conferences its determination to further its [the Jewish National Home in Palestine] development' (Poale Zion 1935). Jewish members of the Labour Party, and members of the Jewish Labour Party, raised the spectre of a socialist homeland in Palestine, linking the cause of Zionism to socialism. This indicates that the Jewish political community in Britain in fact had a valid claim to nationhood in labour discourse, and this needed a home, a territory in the Middle East. Significantly, statements supporting a Jewish homeland were reiterated at the 1936 Labour Party

Conference, amidst pitched battles on the streets of London between the British Union and the political forces opposing its agitation in Jewish areas. Zionism, and hence the removal of Jews to Palestine, was a response to the public order problems created by these battles. In the final analysis Jews would be repatriated to Palestine and order would be restored.[10] This analysis was contested by those in the party who thought support for Palestine 'reactionary' (Hutchinson 1936: 221) and considered that Jews were not a nation, but belonged to the nations in which they lived.

CONCLUSION

By 1936 the Labour Party had assembled a medley of socially undesirable characteristics around its conception of Jews as a racially identified political community. By far the most damaging of these concern the location of Jews as an alien, invading force for political disorder, and an object of social reform. This certainly adds to the field of concepts clustered around race in the discussions concerning Indian independence. Race emerged from the 1930s with a field of concepts constructed around an understanding of commonwealth which focused on citizenship capacity and its field of concepts: order, progress, modernisation and so on, which indicated the value which should be attached to membership of racial categories involving blackness. Race also emerged with a field of concepts constructed around multi-racialism – disorder, invasion and social reform – which attach a particular social value to Jewishness, in the process of defending Englishness. Together, the case studies on India and anti-semitism in East London provide some valuable insights into race as a discursive concept in political discourse, and establish some of the political ground upon which labour addressed postwar race politics.

5

RACE AND RACE RELATIONS IN POSTWAR BRITAIN

This chapter analyses race's field of concepts in the political discourses emerging around black immigration to postwar Britain. Race is still used in constructing political communities around specific purposes, and articulates other concepts in this task. Labour's major focus in postwar race politics was the multi-racial community and the (immigration) processes which created it. Immigration is the subject of the next chapter; this one is concerned with labour's attempts to create a framework for multi-racialism through race relations legislation. This chapter reviews labour's constructions of race between the mid-1950s and the late 1970s and argues that black Britons were given a political significance which was negative, damaging and contributed to black disadvantage. This chapter is mainly an account of official labourism and its dominant themes. Though there is no doubt that some of these positions were contested, there was no significant opposition organised from within the Labour Party at this time. The main forms of opposition were organised around black politics outside the party, and are indicated in journals like *Race and Class* and *Black Liberator*.

The period between the mid-1950s and the late 1970s was characterised by a particular set of concerns in labour's race discourse. The concerns of the 1930s, anti-semitism (understood as a problem of fascism) and decolonisation, were replaced by black commonwealth immigration and race relations as dominant political concerns for labour (Solomos 1989: 48–82). These concerns were about the character of the political community in Britain, under the impact of black migration. Opposition to racism, and public order, were important issues in the mid to late 1970s and are considered in chapter eight. The 1980s produced a shift in political concerns when labour's attention turned from the multi-racial society to focus on the multi-racial party. The debates about black representation are discussed in chapter nine.

COMMONWEALTH

Between the mid-1950s and the late 1970s labour played its part in administering the remaining colonies, and in supervising the decolonisation of large parts of Africa and the Caribbean. No other black dominion received the attention invested in India; and commonwealth, so central in producing labour conceptions of race in the 1930s, had become a marginal political concern by the 1950s. The forms of internationalism and co-operation proffered by the commonwealth remained important to labour, and structured its early dealings with immigration, but the decolonisation process of commonwealth-building was no longer a significant labour issue. Still, reminders of commonwealth and empire are scattered throughout labour's postwar discourse. Labour members, including Brockway, were involved in the Movement for Colonial Freedom (later renamed Liberation) who designated 1960 Africa year, though there is no evidence that colonial freedom any longer excited much activity in the party (see Movement for Colonial Freedom 1960). Labour also had Southern Africa, described as 'a travesty of basic human values and a denial of socialist principles' (Banks 1969: 215) to deal with. Concern about the fate of black Rhodesians was certainly voiced from labour's ranks, but did not excite the same interest as the fate of Indian political prisoners had done in the 1930s (Winnick 1967: 315). The labour government of Harold Wilson was involved militarily in the commonwealth. It responded to the civil war in Nigeria by supplying arms to General Gowan to be used against the Biafrans. 'My Government, our Government is attacked today because it is supplying a sister nation of the commonwealth with arms' (Johnson 1969: 218). Yet this caused little comment in the party. Similar military support was supplied to new commonwealth regimes in Tanzania, Kenya and Uganda to help new African leaders deal with opposition. Clearly labour dealt with some significant colonial and commonwealth issues in the 1950s and 1960s, but they were attributed little significance in a party which had turned its attention to the arrival of black commonwealth citizens in Britain.

SOME GENERAL CONTOURS IN RACE POLITICS

Labour's approach to race in this period was hesitant, and with a heavy emphasis on legislation. Labour chose to deal with race issues through immigration legislation, race relations legislation and, during the anti-facist campaigns, through appeals to public order legislation. Legislation is a forceful mode of statement with some far-reaching implications. Black Britons became objects of legal discourse in the 1960s and 1970s, and were hence construed as a population whose access to Britain must be controlled, and whose rights required special provision. Parliamentary debates on major pieces of legislation affecting immigration and race relations were poorly attended by labour (Ennals 1976: 221), with few prominent members of the parliamentary party, except Joan Lestor and Sid Bidwell, taking an interest.[1] This lack of interest was repeated at party conferences, and in local constituency parties.[2] Labour interest in race issues picked up only in the late 1970s with mobilisation against the National Front. The 1960s and 1970s produced most of the existing legislation on race, and an uneasy silence within the Labour Party.

Labour's silence was the result of opposing sets of political positions and processes, which converged to constrain labour's approach to race. Human equality was integral to socialism.

> It is basic to socialist thought and action that every human being has a right to equal opportunity in economic, in social and in political life. In Britain in the past, this has meant securing for the working class the rights and opportunities that had been available only to a privileged few.
>
> (Labour Party 1967a: 6)

It was clear that the old commitment to a socialist vision of human equality must now include a demand for racial equality, and this was the substance of the Race Relations Working Party report from which this quote is taken. Conflicting with this commitment was labour's history of involvement with race (examined in chapters three and four) from which it is evident that labour attributed some negative and damaging significances to blackness, to immigrants and to multi-racialism. This is supported by hints from speeches at party conference and in parliament, which suggest that labour was active in sustaining in the 1960s and 1970s, the anti-immigrant hostility it had construed in the 1930s (Hynd 1961: 1937, Labour Party 1976: 1001).

> We have to ask ourselves what are the public misapprehensions about immigration. They centre on the worries which concern us within the community generally. I have taken a letter at random from my mailbag today. . . . This woman constituent says: 'You appear to be in favour of unlimited immigrants entering this country. I am not anti-black, but I am anti-overpopulation and hordes of people streaming into England.' She goes on to develop her point quite clearly. This is not a letter stating the demented racist views that we receive in some correspondence.
>
> (Whitehead 1976: 1023–30)

Labour MPs, like the above, would frequently attribute anti-immigrant sentiment to constituents, and no doubt there was some truth in this accusation. But labour was not the political barometer responding to racist pressure that many commentators have suggested (Anwar 1986: 84, Foot 1965: 123).

RACE AND BLACK SKIN

Concepts are construed and given meaning in the political debates in which they occur. They also carry with them meaning acquired in other times and in other contexts. What did race mean in the political debates in the period under consideration? And what does it owe to earlier interpretations? In postwar Britain race was still a concept invoking a range of human distinction. It still had a reference point in human anatomy. The labour Home Secretary in defending the first Race Relations Act (see Home Office 1965a) in parliament spoke of races as having common 'origins . . . or stem from which they proceed'. Races were attributed a reference point in origin and blood (Soskice 1965a: 970–3), invoking historical and genetic membership of categories of the human population. Origins are, of course, constructed forms of historic association; and blood, along with skin is an object of discourse. As in the 1930s, this public declaration on race utilises commonalities construed in historical association and genetic membership.

Debates about race in postwar Britain focused on black people, and it is through these debates that the social significance of blackness was established. Black is a current term of discourse, which became common only in the latter half of the 1970s. Coloured and immigrant were more commonly used at this time (Labour Party 1967b: 3).[3] The term ethnic was not common currency either, though it was used in certain contexts to distinguish between black populations. But at this time black populations were rarely distinguished. They were lumped together because they were seen in terms of their impact on Britain, and not in terms of their different requirements and specificities.[4] Colour and black are both references to skin, race's most significant object in discourse. The physical and visible differences referred to by notions of skin were crucially important in organising debates about race in this period. Skin colour was considered an immutable feature of biology, and hence an unacceptable basis for discrimination: '. . . you cannot change the colour of your skin' (Driberg 1970: 208). Despite this denial of skin as signalling an acceptable basis for social difference, labour itself gave black skin a range of significances in the debates of the time.

Skin has no intrinsic significance. It enters the discourse as a sign of other differences. Skin was widely considered a sign of an alien status (Labour Party 1972a: 21). It was also thought to signify community tensions. 'These [community tensions] can become particularly acute where physical differences of the immigrants are visible, as in the case of coloured people' (Labour Party 1958: 3). The existing state of hostility between the bearers of black and white skin was crucial in defining the quality of the political community. Fear of the kind of racial violence which had erupted in the United States underpinned labour's official warnings and provided a rationale for legislation: 'Unless urgent action is taken to reduce racial discrimination, relations between white people and coloured people here are likely to get dangerously worse' (Labour Party 1967a: 29). Black skin was given other significances too. It was also a sign of social inequalities to be addressed by race relations legislation. The bearers of black skin needed special protection. Black skin was discursively organised and sustained by a field of concepts which stressed community tension, disorder, and the need for special protection. These themes had surfaced around assessments of Indian capacity for citizenship, which suggest that black skin entered postwar politics with a particular range of negative significances which were sustained and recontextualised. This was labour's official position, but there was no prominent opposition to this from within the party itself.

A further examination of labour's race discourse in this period reveals that race's field of concepts retained many of the significances of the 1930s, not all of which were then to do with blackness but which have since been used to sustain the significance of blackness. Black populations, like Jewish people in the 1930s, were a focus for political agitation. There were numerous indications that Asians in particular were victims of racial attack (Adams 1978: 312, Hoey 1978: 316). Racial attack drew certain forms of protest which demanded effective policing, and which dealt with the National Front through street battles, recalling the 1930s clashes with Mosley's Black Shirts. Jewish immigrants to Britain had been conceptualised in terms of disorder. Black commonwealth citizens, whose communities had erupted into disorder around the demand for political freedom, and whose citizenship capacities were questioned by their aptitude for civil order and progress, were recontextualised as a threat to order in Britain. Race also retained in its field of concepts an association with a range of social problems. This is graphically illustrated by labour's dealings with race issues in its existing structure of policy committees in the early 1970s. The Human Rights Sub-Committee (of the Home Policy Committee of the NEC) dealt with what were in fact a range of social problems – 'crime, police, prisons, drugs, race and immigration' (Labour Party 1972b: 1). Race, immigration and black Britons were part of a well rehearsed list of social problems associated with the inner city. Race and the inner city were, and still are, inseparable concepts. By the 1950s the inner city was a black problem (Adney 1970: 206–7), which labour dealt with through a system of inner city funding like the urban programmes.[5] Black Britons, like Jews in the 1930s, were objects of social reform in official labour discourse.

Black immigrant populations had a relationship to poverty

and social reform in labour discourse different from that of Jews in the 1930s. This was because of their association with the commonwealth. Poverty among black immigrants to Britain in the 1950s was understood as the residue of a colonialism which was the subject of critique and arguments to sustain aid to commonwealth countries (Labour Party 1958: 4–5, 7). Poverty was also a sign of diminished political capacity in the debates surrounding the creation of the first black commonwealth country. Black immigrants thus had a double association with poverty, as immigrants and as black commonwealth citizens, an association which problematised, doubly, their capacity for proper forms of political association, and raised anxieties about their impact on the British political community.

RACE RELATIONS

The concept with which race was most commonly associated in official labour discourse was 'relations'. A significant part of labour's approach to race was to take the credit for the achievements of race relations legislation.

> During five and a half years in office the labour government did much to promote integration of immigrants into the community. This contrasts vividly with the inaction of the Conservative Government . . . the Tories failed to take the decisive action so urgently required. . . . With this legislation [1965 Race Relations Act] the Labour Government fulfilled the 1964 election pledge of legislation against acts of racial discrimination and incitement in public places.
>
> (Labour Party 1972a: 25)

What are the implications of the race concept's association with relations? An examination of what was at stake in labourist constructions of relations demonstrates the centrality of labour's concerns about the character of the British political community (nation), in organising its approach to race issues. At the centre of these concerns were once again notions of order. The bearers of black and white skin face each other in mutual incomprehension and hostility in labour's political community. 'The question of whether people of different race can live together in equality and friendship, or whether they will face each other in bloody conflict, is the greatest political and social problem facing the world in the next decade' (Taylor 1976: 216). The 1960s and 1970s were peppered with references to the embitterment of 'relations between races' (Labour Party 1972a: 7), and dire warnings of the consequences 'Unless peoples of different races and colours can learn to live together . . .' (Labour Party 1958: 2). In the late 1950s labour mooted the idea of 'citizens' committees' (Labour Party 1958: 5) to deal with tensions in the political community. But by the 1960s it was seeking solace in race relations legislation.

Race relations was the subject of three major pieces of legislation (1965, 1968 and 1976; see Home Office 1965a, 1968a and 1976), and a focus in postwar labour race politics. Its limitations are well documented (Anwar 1986: 33–5, Ben-Tovim *et al.* 1986: 29, Ben-Tovim and Gabriel 1984: 153–9).[6] Labour's attention to race relations came long after it was raised in parliament in the early 1950s (Brockway 1963: 97–100), and was incremental, each Race Relations Act strengthening the last. Labour's approach to race relations was slow and politically timid, when looked at in terms of its achievements. The legislation achieved limited protection for black people from incitement to racial hatred, from some of the more obvious forms of racial discrimination in allocation procedures, and some recourse to the law. Its powers of enforcement were limited, and its scope only slowly extended to cover employment and housing rights. Race relations legislation remains a statement of labour's inability to deal with racial inequality in a multi-racial society. But race relations legislation was never intended as a defence of black civil rights, neither was it intended to deliver a greater equity in the distribution of social resources. Race relations legislation was labour's attempt to provide a formal legislative framework for multi-racialism, a concept it was unable to entertain in the 1930s.

MULTI-RACIALISM

The options available in the case of Jewish immigration, repatriation and assimilation to the point of invisibility, were no longer feasible. The twin factors of commonwealth and skin laid the problem at Britain's door, and ensured that the new additions to the political community would not, like the Jews, become invisible. From the mid-1950s it was evident that Britain was to be a multi-racial political community, containing visible differences organised around skin colour, and this raised anxieties about what Britishness would, in future, consist of. Fears that multi-racialism would prompt civil disorder as it had in the United States, left labour focusing on a need to reassert certain standards of political conduct.

> Racial discrimination raises moral, social and economic issues. For Socialists the basic problem is by what means can equal opportunity for all, regardless of race or colour be achieved? The outbreak of racial violence in the U.S.A. this summer has demonstrated the need for action to prevent such tragic happenings here. . .
>
> (Labour Party 1967a: 3)

Race relations legislation was a response to a particular set of political concerns focusing on public order and standards of citizenship. It was an attempt to reassert standards of political association and conduct, in a political community which now contained citizens from the black commonwealth.

Concern with public order was the central principle of labour's 1960s race relations legislation. That this legislation was an attempt to secure certain standards of political community under the impact of multi-racialism, and not primarily to guarantee the rights of black citizens, is evident in the parliamentary debates which accompanied the 1965 act. 'The whole purpose of this bill . . . is to bring harmony, harmonious relationships into our community' (Soskice 1965a: 977). Similar concerns were also voiced by the Race Relations Working Party report (Labour Party 1967a: 3). Labour's race relations entered the political arena as an attempt to establish the 'limits of acceptable conduct' (Floud 1965: 970). The legislation set out forms of political association which demanded racial tolerance, and the evasion of political violence. A central concept underlying this discourse was citizenship.

Citizenship featured in three principle senses in the debates surrounding race relations. Firstly, it was a matter of the meaning and value attached to British citizenship under the impact of multi-racialism. Standards of British citizenship were

84

seminal in maintaining Britain's standing among nations. Race relations legislation was a bid to avoid the construction of a dual citizenship, offering black Britons lesser rights.

> It would be a tragedy of the first order if our country with its unrivalled traditions of tolerance and fair play . . . should see the beginnings of the development of a distinction between first and second class citizens and the disfigurement which can arise from inequality of treatment and incitement to feelings of hatred directed to the origins of particular citizens. . .
>
> (Soskice 1965b: 926)

British nationhood required a single citizenship, 'if we are to maintain any sort of world reputation for civilised living and social cohesion' (Jenkins 1966: 8). Nations not observing this requirement, and who allowed race to be a formal focus for different and unequal forms of citizenship (like Rhodesia and South Africa) were a focus for international censure and concern. In so far as black rights were asserted at all in labour discourse, they sustained a particular conception of citizenship in order to secure British superiority over other nations.

Secondly, standards of citizenship requiring orderly conduct were implicitly used to establish a set of norms with which new immigrants were required to comply. Why else would standards of British citizenship be asserted in the context of a multi-racial society, if not against the possibility that its immigrant additions might be the bearers of lower standards of citizenship? Labour had established a second class citizenship for black commonwealth members in its involvement in the decolonisation of India. In negotiating Indian independence Labour insisted on a particular style of political conduct – including the capacity for order, industry, modernisation and so on – and then judged Indians wanting in consenting to such a limited franchise. The political community in Britain and its standards of citizenship were potentially jeopardised by the arrival of black commonwealth immigrants, whose citizenship capacities were suspect. Thirdly, labour's concept of citizenship also had a disciplinary sense in race relations legislation. It provided a mechanism which could curtail the baser instincts of the British electorate. The legislation's attempt to deal with racial hatred offers a reminder that British citizenship also required certain standards of behaviour from the indigenous, or non-immigrant, population. Political violence and incitement to racial hatred were ruled out as valid expressions of collective will. This disciplinarity raised anxieties around the encroachment on the rights of the indigenous population to discriminate, and was the most contentions aspect of the first (1965) Race Relations Act.[7] The Labour Home Secretary had to assure parliament that protecting black citizens from discrimination would 'not unduly inhibit the freedom of private choice' (Soskice 1965b: 935). Nor would it 'inhibit private discussion. It will not inhibit public discussion, but what it forbids is public abuse motivated by the actual intent to incite to hatred' (Soskice 1965b: 939).

The discussion so far in this chapter has concentrated on blackness and its discursive significance. Yet race relations was posed as a problem of community tension, hostility and disorder, arising from the co-existence of black and white in a single multi-racial political community. There was a silence around the social significance of whiteness which, unlike black skin, was not an object of the discourse, though there are occasional references to Englishness. Englishness features in the discourse organised around a common history, and as a reference to character. 'My ancestors did not come over with William the Conqueror' (Winnick 1967: 315).[8] Histories are, of course, constructed around any form of association, and attributed a significance in discourse. References to character were an appeal to a sense of decency: '. . . the vast majority of the British people, who are basically decent, civilised and tolerant . . .' (Benn 10 September 1976: 3). This was fending off other notions of Englishness, those which harbour unpleasant feelings about black immigrants. White skin, Britishness and Englishness in these examples, stood for a common set of historical antecedents, and a national character. In this they are quite different from notions of blackness, which are less positive and do not make use of concepts like history and character. Blackness (mobilising a field of concepts concerning order and social reform in these debates) was a category constructed in labour discourse around its impact on Englishness. This reveals the underlying political objectives of the 1960s and 1970s race relations legislation. It was argued in the case of India that race was a category constructed around specific objectives. Race was constructed in the context of race relations legislation, in order to assert a particular character on behalf of the British political community, to be defended against black immigrants. Labour constructed two oppositional political communities in dealing with multi-racialism. The one was invasive and reconstitutive of the other. This, too, explains the vagueness of conceptions of whiteness and Englishness. Yet again Englishness was not being defined, it was being defended, this time against black immigrants. This theme evident in labour discourse in the 1930s also organised labour's approaches to race in the 1960s and 1970s.

LABOUR'S BLACK CONSTITUENCY

Having constructed blackness in the way in which it did, how did labour relate to the constituency it had construed? Black people were claimed as a labour constituency, but how was this achieved, and how were these claims related to labour's more indigenous constituency, those who would stake a claim to Englishness?

Key labour statements of the time reveal that black immigrants were incorporated into labour's traditional constituency categories, those whose plight was the domain of socialism: workers and the poor. Black immigrants were workers filling gaps in the labour market who 'have brought us their skills and labour which we badly need in building up our economy' (Soskice 1965b: 943). They were also trade unionists and potentially members of the party, 'our brothers' in struggle (Larkin 1967: 313). Using the worker category it was easy for black immigrants to be claimed in any struggle for social justice: '. . . our socialist philosophy, our commitment to social justice, includes the black worker as surely as it includes the white worker' (Lestor 1972: 158).

But the inclusion of black Britons in labour's traditional constituencies was problematic. Labour had actively constructed a particular distinctiveness around blackness in the debates of the 1960s and 1970s, as this chapter has demonstrated. If black people were a distinctive category for analysis and concern, could they then be collapsed into the categories worker and the poor, when it came to construing constituencies and their political objectives? If worker was a racially constructed category, could it at the same time be sustained as a unitary constituency, by giving it a single objective: a struggle for greater social justice? Here we are confronted with the limited nature of labourist frameworks. Labour was unable to deal with racial equality as a separate issue; it had to be incorporated into labour's framework of class and trade union politics. This imposes all sorts of constraints on any demand for racial equality which can be sustained by this framework.

The problem of labour's constituency is yet more complex. Labour did not just construct worker as a racialised category, and then proceed to overlook this in developing political strategies and objectives. Labour constructed black and white workers as having contradictory interests. Black workers feature in labour discourse as being in competition with white workers for resources, adding to the poverty of the inner city, and hence the generally stressed lives of the white working class. This is the implication of all the special inner city funding and the thinking behind the support labour gave to dispersal policies for black immigrants in the 1960s.

> Any member who has an immigration problem within his constituency knows full well that there is a deep resentment within the working class section of the community at the social problems that follow in the wake of an influx of coloured immigrants.
>
> (Binns 1965: 1003)

This kind of statement is not at all surprising, and was not an outside political pressure from the constituencies to which labour had to respond. Labour actively constructed the significance of blackness in terms which made it an oppositional political community confronting Englishness, and requiring a defence of Englishness. Small wonder then that these oppositional political categories should be understood to be in competition for scarce resources. Labour was not just responding to racism, it was actively creating its own forms of racial disadvantage in political discourse. In the 1960s and 1970s it did this in constructing notions of multi-racialism through race relations legislation.

CONCLUSION

Labour's construction of the race concept in official statements between the mid-1950s and the late 1970s drew upon a field of concepts which articulated notions of disorder, social disadvantage and a range of social problems focused on the inner city. Black immigrants to Britain were thus contextualised as being an object of social reform, and associated with standards of citizenship which placed civil order in Britain at risk. In general, labour constructed the significance of blackness in terms which were likely to disadvantage and place in question the capacities of black British citizens. It need not have done this. It need not have relied so closely on concepts it construed around race in the 1930s, in its encounter with commonwealth and Jewishness in East London. Labour had developed a concept of citizenship through its dealings with race relations, though this was not explicitly stated, which could have been used to support a notion of black citizenship rights. Labour missed this opportunity to address black rights, and instead provided a juridical framework for multi-racialism. Multi-racialism was obviously a concept which still made labour uneasy, and which privileged standards of order and citizenship. Labour did more than respond to popular racism, it sustained explicit expressions of racism within the party, by giving it political weight and credibility. It did this by generating its own negative assessments of the political significance of blackness, around concerns about the viability of a multi-racial society which was clearly there to stay.

6

LABOUR AND IMMIGRATION FROM THE 1950s TO THE 1990s

Immigration is a uniquely significant political issue. A recurring theme in British postwar politics, it is the subject of four major pieces of legislation,[1] numerous changes in the rules which govern its procedures, and some intensive arguments about human rights. As a subject of fierce controversy, it is rarely absent at general election time. Immigration laws' impact on the lives of those who have migrated to Britain cannot be overstated. Immigration laws and their procedures have determined who may enter Britain, and on what conditions. They have violated bodies, divided families, and frustrated overseas, particularly black, visitors to Britain.

This chapter addresses some key issues. What does the term immigrant mean? Like other concepts, immigrant is given meaning and force through the contexts in which it is significant. In the period covered by this chapter immigrant was a political category which was significantly reconstructed, through changes in immigration legislation, and the debates which surrounded these changes. These shifts are important because the term immigrant was used to distinguish and exclude populations, and we are, in this chapter, interested in mapping labour's contribution to these processes. Like the last chapter, this is concerned with an overall mapping of concepts, by examining dominant official themes. The Labour Party itself was not an important site of opposition to official themes. Opposition to labour's immigration policy was organised outside the party, in pressure groups like the Joint Council for the Welfare of Immigrants, and the Commission for Racial Equality. This chapter is centrally concerned with how immigrant was an object of labour discourse, what it meant and what part it played in construing Britain as a political community. Some attention has already been given to the issue of labour's postwar political community in examining multi-racialism in the context of labour's race relations legislation. This chapter will show what concerns organised around immigration add to this.

Immigration is a central concept in postwar labour discourses concerned with race, dominating and organising labour's output from the 1950s, and is still significant in the 1990s. Labour's report of the working party on race relations, for example, is actually all about 'immigrants' and the 'coloured population' (Labour Party 1967a: 24). The 1960s also produced a flurry of information papers on immigration (Labour Party 1968a, 1968b). The majority of official labour statements concerning race issues in the 1970s were also preoccupied with immigration, for example, 'Citizenship, Immigration and Integration' (Labour Party 1972a). Immigration was the subject of various information papers on race in the 1980s, taking the Conservative Party to task for its approach (Labour Party 1980a, 1980b, 1981a, 1983a, 1983b). Immigration was a way of speaking about race, and has some significant implications which need exploration.

IMMIGRANT AND IMMIGRATION IN DISCOURSE

Immigration was one of race's field of concepts in the 1930s. In the context of Jewishness, immigrant acquired an association with a field of social pathologies which included disorder, social reform and a focus on the inner city (see chapter four). These significances re-emerged in a reorganised form in the era of large-scale black immigration to Britain, so that black immigrants acquired these significances. Additionally black immigrants were commonwealth citizens whose capacity for proper political association was placed in question. This was evident in labour's 1960s and early 1970s approach to multi-racialism (see chapter five). Immigration was a black issue by the 1950s, and hence labour's race discourse is characterised by a particular constellation of the concepts black, immigrant and race, and it is this which makes this period distinctive (Labour Party 1967a: 29).[2]

Immigrant is both a concept generated and arranged in

discourses, producing descriptions of a population, and it is also a discursive device. That is, immigrant is an idea which is used in a particular way. In this chapter we are interested in what it means as a concept and in how it was used. As with other concepts, we can establish its meaning or significance by determining its associated concepts in discourse, and the purposes for which it was employed. Immigrant is a concept which offers a description of a population. Its general significance is that it stresses exteriority, alien origins and a sense of non-belonging to the political community, and of course, it entered the discourse in the 1950s with a range of associated concepts. The concept immigrant distinguishes and differentiates populations by construing the polarities of indigenousness[3] and exteriority. Immigrant indicates the status of a population in relation to the political community as a whole. It indicates a population with exterior origins, whose access requires scrutiny, and may be denied. The claims of immigrants on a political community need to be established, and the establishment of claims is circumscribed by (immigration and nationality) law. Laws and the practices they sustain are also modes of statement, and may be analysed as discourse.

What does indigenousness consist of? This will be established through an examination of the discourse around immigration. But first some general observations. It was noted in chapter five that reference to indigenousness may include a statement of commonality around a history or character, as a basis for community. This is usually a statement of Englishness. It was also noted in chapter five that statements of Englishness in race discourse, are of course, prompted by the presence of immigrants, and take on the status of something which is being defended. Indigenous populations do not have their claims to membership of the political community scrutinised in the same way as immigrants. Indigenous claims to membership are not mediated by formal immigration controls. Labour's notions of indigenousness are important in establishing an understanding of the nature of the political community into which immigrants are received, and its political aspirations or 'will'. It will be argued that labour generated a particular notion of indigenousness, in its involvement with immigration, which construed constituencies whose political aspirations had then to be serviced through immigration restrictions. Constituencies, of course, are the component populations of a political community with identifiable and representable interests.

Exteriority is established against indigenousness: the one gives meaning to, and sustains the other. This chapter is concerned with immigrants whose entry to Britain preceded permanent settlement, and who originated from the black commonwealth, as this was the population at which immigration restriction was aimed. Access to Britain for these populations was not mediated by controls before 1962, but they were still popularly referred to as immigrants. Immigration controls stipulate who may enter Britain, and on what conditions. They are sustained by nationality laws[4] which establish the basis upon which membership of a political community may be acquired. The boundaries established by immigration and nationality legislation have been redrawn many times in the postwar period, and these are important discourses in generating immigrant as a social category. Immigrant has a content in a field of concepts which will be identified, as the discourse is examined in this chapter. In a general sense separation and exclusion are some of the most important effects generated around the concept immigrant. It is unsurprising, therefore, that discussions about immigration are linked with popular feelings about blackness, the extent to which black people are welcomed in Britain, and their human rights respected. To some extent this accounts for the continued significance of immigration as a political issue, long after black Britons have ceased to be immigrants. The treatment of immigrants provides an important commentary on the character of a political community, and its standards of conduct.

COMMONWEALTH IMMIGRANTS

Labour responded to black immigration to Britain in the early 1950s by invoking a conception of commonwealth. 'Britain has become symbolically and practically the heart of the Commonwealth. To an important extent this is due to the fact that all Commonwealth citizens are welcomed in our midst' (Labour Party 1958: 2). This shows that commonwealth was a key concept in constructing a notion of immigrant, and in giving it a

93

significance. Commonwealth invoked a form of connection to Britain, and provided the rationale by which black immigrants were given access to the British political community. It was access which distinguished commonwealth from alien immigrants, who were required to negotiate the 1905 Aliens Act and the 1948 British Nationality Act.[5] Under these two pieces of legislation commonwealth immigrants were effectively British, in the sense of having a right to enter and live in Britain without restriction. They were not of course regarded as British in any other sense. Commonwealth membership connected black immigrants to Britain, but commonwealth could not indefinitely sustain the right of commonwealth citizens to live in Britain. It is evident from debates at the time that this was not the central political objective around which notions of commonwealth were deployed. What is interesting is that commonwealth sustained the right of free access to Britain for commonwealth citizens for as long as it did. Despite protestations to the effect that 'all commonwealth citizens are welcome in our midst. If our position is to continue, the welcome must be wholehearted and unreserved' (Labour Party 1958: 2) and 'We are firmly convinced that any form of British legislation limiting commonwealth immigrants to this country would be disastrous to our status in the commonwealth and to the confidence of the commonwealth peoples' (Labour Party 1957: 2–3), labour was never committed to sustaining the right of commonwealth citizens to live in Britain, even in the 1950s. Even those who claimed that it would be dishonourable to 'close the door against our own British brethren' (Royle 1961: 1978) supported collaboration among commonwealth governments on the issue of the limitation of the number of 'coloured' immigrants arriving in Britain still. The commons debate on immigration control early in 1961 contained few references to commonwealth except as a mechanism for restriction (*Parliamentary Debates: Official Report* 1961: 1929–2024). Labour had always officially supported the limitation of immigrants entering Britain, but preferred agreement, and increased aid to commonwealth countries, to controls.

If commonwealth was not a mode of connection whose primary purpose was to sustain black immigration to Britain, what then was its central purpose? How did commonwealth function as a discursive device? As well as connecting black immigrants to Britain, commonwealth membership also secured their distinctiveness and, later, their exclusion. This point becomes clearer if we examine labourist notions of commonwealth invoked in debates around immigration. What did commonwealth mean in labour immigration discourse? How was it generated and sustained as a concept? What significance did it attach to the concept immigrant? And what was its central purpose as a discursive device? These issues are addressed by deconstructing commonwealth.

Commonwealth was symbolic for labour. It symbolised a set of political principles, and a particular vision of Britain and its standing among nations. Commonwealth represented the possibility of international harmony, peace and co-operation, key concepts in defining a socialist foreign policy. Labour's official vision of commonwealth is expressed thus:

> The New Commonwealth which has grown up since 1945, represents the greatest multi-racial association the world has ever known. Yet the commonwealth is continually sensitive about race relations. Failure in these relations can destroy all hopes of peace and international friendship. Unless peoples of different races and colours can learn to live together in harmony, the future of our children in this rapidly shrinking world will be one of extreme danger. The commonwealth has a unique opportunity to create racial understanding, confidence and co-operation.
>
> (Labour Party 1958: 2)

Commonwealth offered labour the prospect of a multi-racial community in which Britain would have a central part. This assertion of multi-racialism could not have referred to Britain, but a multi-racialism safely spread around the world, for, as we established in the last chapter, labour was still nervous about multi-racialism even in the late 1960s. The multi-racialism of commonwealth was important in creating a labour-image of Britain. It embodied labour's claim to distinctiveness in foreign policy.

Labour did not just support the commonwealth, it took credit for it. 'The transformation of the old British Empire into the first inter-racial Commonwealth of free nations was the supreme achievement of the labour government' (Labour Party 1959: 278).

More important, commonwealth was a monument to Britain's standing among other nations. 'Socialists place the development of our multi-racial commonwealth community first in our vision of Britain's place in world affairs' (Labour Party 1959: 278). Labour's commonwealth in the 1950s did for labourism what empire did for conservatism. It allowed the staking of Britain's place in world affairs. Though replacing conquest with co-operation, this was still an assertion of British superiority over other nations, through the exercise of British influence in the dominions. Thus the central purpose of commonwealth was to assert labourism and its distinctive contribution to British politics. For if labour's construction of commonwealth had been intended as welcome to immigrants, then it would have been more positive about multi-racialism, and more vociferous in asserting the fact that commonwealth immigrants were British citizens. Foot's (1965: 191) suggestion, that the commonwealth ideal was sold for votes in restricting black immigration, offers a misreading of the significance of commonwealth. The commonwealth ideal had never been intended as a defence of black immigration to Britain.

The concept commonwealth in fact establishes the political distinctiveness of immigrants, and not a Britishness which could indefinitely serve as the basis for a claim to access to Britain. A closer examination of its use as a discursive device reveals that commonwealth was actually used in staking out two distinctive political communities, one indigenous and the other immigrant. This purpose is revealed in a number of labour statements in the 1950s. Commonwealth immigrants came from 'countries which have been ruled by Britain for centuries, frequently to the benefit of the British people' (Labour Party 1958: 3). They were characterised by their association with colonial domination (Henderson 1961: 1960). Labour (1958: 3) acknowledged that being a subject, rather than a beneficiary, of empire created forms of poverty and a pressure to migrate to Britain in the first place; 'the responsibility for there being no secondary factories in Jamaica in 1955 rests with this government' (Brockway 1961: 1997). Commonwealth immigrants were thus construed as exploited, impoverished and displaced. Their distinctiveness was further organised by their acquisition of independence from Britain. The significance attached to black citizenship in these processes of independence (discussed in detail in chapter three) contextualised black immigrants as a population whose capacity for proper political association was anyway placed in doubt. And this underlying assumption took on particular significances in debates surrounding immigration in the 1950s and 1960s. A significant set of concepts associated with commonwealth immigrants in the late 1950s and early 1960s sustained the interpretation of immigrants as a particularly dislocated form of British citizen. Cultural and linguistic unfamiliarity produced its own forms of 'strangeness and stress' (Labour Party 1958: 3), prompting similar fears in the communities in which immigrants settled.

The distinctiveness bestowed upon immigrants differentiated them from, and placed them in opposition to, the indigenous population. Commonwealth immigrants were construed in such negative and damaging terms, that their impact upon the nation could not possibly have been seen by labour as beneficial. This point is sustained by the examination of labour's approach to multi-racialism in chapter five. Indigenousness, in discourses concerned with immigration, was construed in terms of being the beneficiary of empire, racially prejudiced and in need of education to promote racial tolerance (Labour Party 1958: 3). Whilst it was undoubtedly necessary for labour to address these issues, labour retained this notion of indigenousness as a significant political calculation. This construction of indigenousness accorded a prominence to the political demands of this constituency, which were about exclusion. When in 1964 labour agreed that immigration controls were the way to restrict immigration, it was bowing to a political logic constructed through its own accounts of the significance of immigrants, the meaning of indigenousness, and the political requirements of the indigenous population.

Placed in this context labour's agreement to immigration controls is not surprising. It is, however, the result of political choices, and not inevitability. Despite weak opposition to official policy on immigration, labour need not have constructed indigenousness in this way; it could have appealed to a sense of decency as Benn did later (see chapter five). Labour effectively construed a concept of immigrant which placed in jeopardy the character of the political community of nation. Immigrant was more than an oppositional category constructed against indigenousness, it was invasive of indigenousness. Indigenousness and immigrant were construed in ways which required immigration controls. Immigrant need not have been given these significances, which made exclusion and restriction the only possible outcomes, although admittedly, alternate and more positive images of immigrants were weakly developed in British politics at this time. Labour's approval of immigration controls in 1964 signalled nothing more dramatic than a change in political strategy, favouring controls over other methods of restriction. The major shift for labour in the 1960s was not the decision to implement controls, but the displacement of commonwealth as a central concept structuring the understanding of immigrant, by the establishment of immigrants as workers in the early 1960s.

WORKER IMMIGRANTS

Commonwealth, central in defining immigrants in labour discourse in the 1950s, survived into the early 1960s when it was displaced by the linking of immigrants with work. Although in the 1960s the Labour Party (1962: 197) was still taking credit for the multi-racial commonwealth, this was now jeopardised by 'racial hatred', which could be dealt with through race relations legislation, and not jeopardised immigration controls. This shows that labour's commonwealth survived immigration control, and that it was a plastic concept, which could be deployed around a multiplicity of political objectives, and not just access to Britain. Like commonwealth in the 1950s, the notion of worker in the 1960s sustained a distinctiveness for immigrants, the logic of which was exclusion. The Conservative Party's 1962 Commonwealth Immigrants Act redefined access to Britain, removing the automatic right of entry for commonwealth citizens, and linking immigration to labour needs. The internal needs of the British labour market now mediated access to Britain, and the commonwealth officially became a viable source of mobile labour. Commonwealth citizens were no longer British subjects with a right to live in Britain, they were workers and their dependent families, limited by employment vouchers issued by the Ministry of Labour. In future access to Britain was to be conditional on skill shortages and labour needs. This was a major shift redefining the relationship between Britain and the commonwealth. The political community of commonwealth was ruptured by a notion of labour market, and the union of British brethren became a pool of mobile labour.[6] Labour's opposition to the 1962 act was organised around objecting to the Act's effect in operating a colour bar (Royle 1961: 1971), the assertion that controls were the wrong way to go about the business of exclusion, and that it thwarted the needs of industry. Commonwealth obligations and the claims which could be made upon them did not have the centrality they are often accorded, and were not anyway claims invoking a unity as is often assumed (Ben-Tovim and Gabriel 1984: 148, Foot 1965: 191).

Well before the 1962 Immigration Act, the claims of commonwealth as an expression of international brotherhood had been eclipsed by a demand for labour. The TUC had been involved in recruitment campaigns for London transport in the 1950s, and the early 1960s parliamentary debates on immigration refer to the 'needs of certain industries' and 'employment policy' (Parkin 1961: 1947), showing that labour's defence of free access to Britain was predominantly construed around labour shortages, and not the historical obligations of empire. 'It is grotesque to suggest that there should be a bar to immigration on the terms suggested by the honourable gentleman [Cyril Osborne] when we know that certain industries are short of labour'(Parkin 1961: 1948). By the time labour was declaring 'The Labour Party accepts the need for control over the number of commonwealth immigrants entering this country [as it had in fact done throughout the 1950s]. The vital question is not control itself but how this control should be operated' (Labour Party 1964: 1). Labour had already accepted that immigrants were workers. By 1965 labour was itself operating a form of control premised on this redefinition of commonwealth citizens through Wilson's white paper (Immigration from the Commonwealth 1965) which had some important implications, excluding immigrants more effectively than the Conservatives' controls. If immigrants were workers whose entry to Britain was permitted by labour shortages, then, in the absence of any other right to entry, their access could be disallowed when there were no longer shortages. Although serving the needs of the labour market remains a reason for immigration, its significance as a concept organising an understanding of immigration has declined. Labour market needs are anyway open to wide interpretation, and can radically change, as any immigration policy based on this claim must ultimately recognise.

The reconceptualisation of immigrants as workers from the commonwealth and not simply a union of British brethren, sustained the concerns of the 1950s that immigrants imposed on scarce resources. The demand that immigration should take account of the effect on the 'social and economic difficulties of this country' (Parkin 1961: 1948–9) was a fairly typical response of this time. This theme of the social difficulties posed by immigrants, and organised around Britain's capacity to absorb, was popular among labour MPs, who vociferously asserted the prior claims of their constituents, in the context of immigration debates. But arguments about pressures on resources can only have a meaning in the context of distinguishing populations from each other, and establishing a primacy of claims. Clearly, for labour, immigrants were a distinctive population whose impact on the indigenous population was of questionable value, and who had a lesser claim than others to society's scarce resources. Against this were a minority who saw immigrants as a challenge to policy-makers, and who did not accept that capacity-to-absorb arguments were linked to the logic of exclusion (Henderson 1961: 1961). This was the small voice of labour opposition to control and social resources arguments. It did not become a well developed opposition to official policy, but it existed within the limits of labourism in the early 1960s.

Immigrant workers were distinguished from indigenous workers through arguments about social pressure, and prior claims on resources. But an examination of labour statements in the 1960s also indicates that immigrant workers were differentiated as the bearers of lesser standards of development. Just as commonwealth sustained some significant differences between immigrant and indigenous populations, so too did the reconceptualisation of immigrants as workers. The significances attached to the black commonwealth did not disappear when commonwealth ceased to be a central principle in constructing notions of political community, under the impact of immigration. Some of the significances of commonwealth transferred to the conceptualisation of immigrants as workers, which came with the changes in immigration controls. Black worker immigrants were a focus for labour anxieties concerning their impact upon the political community, and these anxieties were organised by an understanding of development. Although concerns with development were not explicitly stated in an official sense, they were stated publicly (through parliament) and because no attempt was made by labour to disassociate itself from these conceptions, they must be interpreted as falling within the limits of labourism. Development operated as a discursive device for distinguishing indigenous from immigrant workers. It corresponds with a readiness by labour to operate exclusion through controls (Ben-Tovim and Gabriel 1984: 148) and contains some damaging implications in construing immigrant as a concept.

Notions of development focused on health. Fears of bodily contact and contagion are explicit in statements like the following: 'their ideas of personal hygiene are absolutely different from ours. They have no idea of our public health regulations ...' (Binns 1965: 1005). This was a reference to Pakistanis, made in the context of supporting the Race Relations Bill of 1965, and adds support to the earlier contention in chapter five that labour was nervous about multi-racialism in the 1960s. Immigrants in this assessment were diseased and likely to infect an indigenous population, who were accustomed to higher standards of health and hygiene. Notions of development also focused on the state of social, economic and political conditions in countries sourcing immigration. Labour parliamentary references to immigrants as 'tribesmen' who came 'straight from the tribal villages of Pakistan' (Binns 1965: 1005) invoked terms of anthropological discourse, to emphasize differences in living conditions and expectations between the immigrant and the indigenous population, and also to express concerns about the poverty of immigrants (Lyon 1976b: 221). Literacy, education and competence in English were also concerns linked to a notion of development. A trade unionist involved in recruiting for London Transport in the Caribbean commented that many immigrants had been unsuitable for employment in Britain because of their 'educational standards and their knowledge of English' (Johnson 1965: 216). These popular concerns were

101

reflected in official policy in the channelling of funding into schools and English language programmes, through special funding arrangements like the urban programmes.

These notions of development were extended in the 1970s to forms of domestication with the arrival of Ugandan Asians. Labour women offered crash courses in English, child care and domestic management around the settlement camps. 'The pioneer women of Great Britain have proposed a resolution urging local women's sections to help educate immigrant women in their own homes. It suggests that they could be taught the English language, child care and domestic management in this way' (*Labour Weekly* 4 February 1972: 10). This pioneer spirit invokes a missionary zeal, which recalls the manner in which labour set about establishing 'proper' trade unions in India in the 1930s. Generally, although the arrival of Ugandan Asians was met with the same kind of pressure on resources arguments and defensiveness of the indigenous poor against what were seen as wealthy refugees, the Ugandan Asians were seen as a more professional and hence developed immigrant group. They were considered more easily absorbable into British society and provide evidence that even in the later 1960s and early 1970s the concept immigrant was not uniform.[7] East African Asians were not worker immigrants, but refugees with no other citizenship, reminders that the forms of connection to Britain construed around commonwealth had never been properly settled. The case of East African Asians and the significances attached to the concept immigrant in this context, underlines the significance of notions of development in organising an understanding of immigration and its impact on the British political community.

Labour concerns about the capacities of the immigrant worker population for development vividly recall concerns of the 1930s, and labour's construction of Indian citizenship around those populations deemed capable of supporting the development process. In the 1960s labourism was able to sustain these highly damaging and negative significances of immigrants as a population whose development was in question. It sustained them officially by responding to them, offering tacit support through its policies of dispersal and assimilation (Wilson 1968: 1155–6), and through its readiness to implement controls. Immigrants were to be excluded where there was no labour need, and to be dispersed through the nation to minimalise their impact on the political community. This is clear evidence that whether through conceptualising immigrants using a notion of commonwealth, or using the notion of worker, labour constructed a significance for immigrants which posed them as an invasive and oppositional political community to indigenousness. This was a parallel process to what was happening through race relations legislation discussed in chapter five.

PATRIALITY

It was a labour government which reconstructed immigration away from commonwealth and labour needs. From 1968 primary immigration required a more 'substantial connection' (Labour Party 1968a: 4) to Britain. The concept of patriality[8] required the demonstration of a close family connection, as birth and territory became the new forms of qualification around which the claims of immigrants would be organised. The effects of this act in restricting immigration to Britain, in instituting specific forms of racial exclusion, and in retracting the promises of the past, is well documented and widely protested against. The 1968 Commonwealth Immigrants Act, however, maintained the right of families to join immigrants settled in Britain in law, if not in terms of the practices of immigration officers (Moore and Wallace 1975: 57–76). The 1971 Immigration Act, [9] which extended the notion of patriality set out in 1968 by labour, is still the mainstay of British immigration policy. This removed the claims of black commonwealth citizens to be immigrants to Britain and completed a process set in train by labour which, in construing immigrant and indigenousness as separate and antagonistic political communities, legislatively and most effectively defended the intolerant from the undesirable.

Although labour subsequently regretted patriality, it favoured the kind of immigration restriction which it offered. Summing up official labour policy on immigration in the 1970s is Home Secretary Roy Jenkins (1976: 97): 'I am determined, and I shall be for as long as I am in my present office, to apply strict immigration controls fairly, to uphold the rules, to root out illegal immigration and to deal with overstaying.' Patriality secured a quest for 'limited and low figures' (Jenkins 1973: 1487).

This was necessary because 'In a small and highly populated country there is a limit to the number of immigrants we can absorb' (Rees 1976: 218). Official labour statements throughout the 1970s anxiously repeat the immigration figures, as though immigration were a major political problem, and correspond to concerns over illegal immigration to Britain at this time.[10] There was some opposition to these preoccupations. Others in the party considered it wrong to play the 'numbers game' (Lestor 1976: 74). But in order to effectively apply this argument, it would have been necessary to challenge the field of concepts construed around immigrant, blackness and race. This did not happen, at least not in the Labour Party. If numbers were labour's priority then it deserved patriality, and had anyway significantly contributed to the political debate which produced it. It had construed a community of indigenous Britons who required immigration control. It was bound then to service this demand.

By the time the 1981 British Nationality Act arrived, bringing citizenship into line with the right of abode, and removing the citizenship rights of those born in Britain but who did not have one British-born parent, immigrant was a highly restricted category in political discourse. It was so restrictive that primary immigration from the black commonwealth was no longer possible; there were only limited provisions for worker-immigrants, and these did not favour commonwealth citizens. Commonwealth is retained in a symbolic sense in this Act, a testament to its power as an organising concept in postwar immigration debates and legislation.[11] Forms of restriction which have occurred since 1981 and which labour now contests, have consisted of further erosion of the rights of immigrants settled in Britain to be joined by their families.

The 1988 Immigration Act ensures that future commitments to dependants of immigrants from black commonwealth countries are contingent upon demonstrating adequate levels of financial support 'without recourse to public funds', and conforming to 'acceptable' patterns of marriage and family life (UK Immigrants' Advisory Service 1988: 39). This is an attack on the poor, historically the object of immigration control, whose right to family life is mediated by their ability to provide for their dependants in a society where racist allocation procedures make this all the more difficult. Unprecedented levels of social and cultural conformity are now demanded of immigrants and their dependants as access to Britain has never been more strictly defined. The 1988 Immigration Act is an attack on those whose patterns of family life are governed by other principles. It stops dependants of polygamous marriages immigrating to Britain. As one labour MP commented in respect of the new measures:

> All the Bill's provisions are unpleasant or unnecessary. I shall not bother to go into the provision to stop the 'great plague of polygamy' that is apparently sweeping the country. . . . Even on the Government's figures there are only twenty-five cases a year, and there is no need for legislation to deal with that problem.
>
> (Abbott 1987: 815)

Labour was not directly responsible for this measure but, as this chapter has demonstrated, labour played a significant part in sustaining and giving political direction to immigration control in postwar politics.

LABOUR AND IMMIGRATION IN THE 1990s

Labour's approach to immigration has helped produce a black population, settled in Britain, who came when immigrant meant something else. Once defined as commonwealth citizens or as workers, they have no stake in patriality. They are the victims of all forms of racial exclusion and inequality, and they are entitled to interpret moves to restrict immigration as a statement about their status in Britain. As a black MP put it, the purpose of the 1988 Immigration Act was to 'make people feel they are unwanted' (Abbott 1987: 817). This distinction between the welcome and the unwanted is one which immigration legislation has always made in constructing the concept immigrant. Immigrant is a way of designating the unwanted, the undesirable, those whose impact on the political community must be monitored and challenged. Immigration legislation and its procedures are instrumental in constructing lesser rights for black citizens. Immigrants and those of recent immigrant origins have a highly qualified right to family life. Their right to free movement in and out of the country, and to bring in their friends and family for visits, is challenged by the practices of immigration officers and the small print in the immigration rules. Differential rights have effectively constructed a dual citizenship. There are those who have an unchallenged right to live in Britain, come and go as they please, and receive overseas visits from friends and relatives. These citizens are white. Then there are those who at one point immigrated to Britain, who would no longer be allowed to do so, whose right to be joined by family members is scrutinised, whose cultural practices are challenged, and whose visitors are likely to be detained at ports of entry. These citizens are black (Lyon 1976a: 57). These differential rights are constructed around the distinctiveness of immigrants established in labour discourse on immigration. Labour played a central part in establishing a conceptualisation of immigrant and the political community which allows this particular form of dual citizenship.

What will labour do about the situation it has produced through its dealings with immigration? A shift in labour thinking on immigration is evident and the political context for this is sketched in throughout the remainder of this study. Labour has been highly critical of postwar immigration policy (Messina 1989: 141). It largely refuses to admit its own responsibility in developing that policy. But it has now declared its intention to do something about immigration, and this is interpreted by Messina as disentangling itself from the bipartisan consensus which characterises race politics. From the early 1980s we are repeatedly assured in official labour statements that the repeal of the 1971 Immigration Act and the 1981 Nationality Act 'will be among the highest priorities for the next Labour Government' (Labour Party 1987: 5).

> Public debate about immigration should be about the promotion of international contacts; about our economic need for workers from other countries; about ensuring that families can be united. The basic principle which should underline British immigration law – and which runs through the Labour Party policies set out here – is that every citizen, and everyone settled here, should be entitled to equal treatment regardless of sex or race. . . . The next Labour Government will undertake a fundamental reform of nationality and immigration law. It will repeal the 1971 Immigration Act and the 1981 British Nationality Act and

replace them with legislation which will not discriminate on grounds of race or sex, which will fully respect human rights, and of which a multiracial society will have no reason to be ashamed. . . . This does not mean that Britain can or should abandon all control of immigration in a world of economic inequality in which every country has some form of immigration control.

(National Executive Committee 1982: 1)

The lobby demanding immigration reform in the labour party is no longer insignificant as it was in the 1960s.

But what will labour replace these laws with? What will be its stance on immigration? Labour has promised that existing legislation is to be replaced by policies which are non-discriminatory on grounds of race and gender, and which respect human rights, obligations to refugees, a need for foreign workers and international contact (National Executive Committee 1982: 1). What this will mean in practice is not clear. Labour claims its new Nationality Act will define as British those whose claim is by birth (in Britain) alone and removed by the 1981 Act; commonwealth citizens here before 1973 who wish to register as British (a right which was also removed by the 1981 Nationality Act); and those married to British citizens of either sex. Labour also promises clear and less ambivalent criteria for the acquisition of British citizenship, for those who are not otherwise entitled to it, though it has so far been unable to say what these might be. Labour is also publicly committed to a less harsh definition of dependants in a defence of family life, to admitting workers for occupations where there are shortages, and to respecting the rights of foreign visitors, students and refugees.

There is no doubt that these would be welcome improvements, should they ever be implemented. But there is clearly no intention to reconstruct immigration on principles other than patriality, as defining access to the British political community. Labour offers no other principle upon which immigration might be based. Given the lack of a statement of principle, and an apparent unwillingness to do more than tinker with existing forms of restriction, we might be sceptical of achieving any real improvements in this important area of citizenship rights for black Britons. We might also be sceptical about improvements in the rights of those who once had British citizenship. Demands from Hong Kong, that the British citizenship of Hong Kong residents be upheld when the colony becomes part of China, were met with a restatement of the numbers and crowded island argument. Canada, at least, extended a commonwealth welcome to those from Hong Kong who have certain capital assets. This may not be a very egalitarian principle, but it is a principle, and not the blanket exclusion invoked by Britain. Labour's difficulty with principle is that, historically, immigration control was constructed around principles which required the separation and defence of the indigenous population from immigrants. This principle is no longer tenable, especially as the indigenous population now includes a settled black population with immigrant roots, now firmly entrenched in a multi-racial community, which is here to stay. Labour needs to construct an immigration policy which recognises this fact, and the civil rights of black members who form an important part of this community.

CONCLUSION

This chapter has demonstrated that labour played a central part in constructing immigrant as a political category, around some negative and undesirable characteristics, which draw upon and sustain notions of racial difference and the significance of blackness. From the 1950s labour constructed the logic for the exclusion of immigrants, through its notion of commonwealth and commonwealth workers. It introduced the notion of patriality, and welcomed the low immigration figures it produced. The result was the construction of a political community in which racial equality is impossible. It is time that labour gave an unambivalent message to those whom it has, historically, designated unwanted, by doing something about immigration which will defend, and not attack, the citizenship rights of black Britons.

7

ANTI-RACISM IN THE 1930s

Labour's understanding of race and its emergence in a range of political issues has so far formed the substance of this study. This chapter, and the next, deal with labour's anti-racism, its substance, implications and political boundaries. This chapter reviews labour's understanding of the political problems in East London in the 1930s, focusing on anti-semitic agitation and its forms of address. What did labour's earliest approaches to anti-racism[1] consist of? How did labour defend Jewish residents of East London from attack? What were the political conditions (conditions of emergence) in which particular kinds of anti-racist strategies, and not others, were possible? What kinds of strategies were rejected by labour in these processes? And what were the implications of this for labour's representation of constituencies organised with reference to racial difference? This chapter establishes the terms in which labour was able to defend Jewish populations, and its implications for the later defence of black populations in the 1970s. At the centre of this is an assessment of labour as a force for an anti-racist politics.

Labour constructed Jewishness as a distinctive, racial category around a range of social pathologies (see chapter four). Officially at least, Jewishness was an object of racial attack, associated with poverty, social reform, over-exploited labour and immigration control. Jews focused public anxieties about invasion and political disorder. This construction of Jewishness jeopardised the social fabric, and its political traditions of order and social progress. Jewishness in the 1930s, like blackness in the 1950s and 1960s, was construed around a central principle, which was concerned with the defence of the nation and its character as a political community, in the face of contact with immigrant populations defined with reference to racial distinctiveness. How then would labour approach the business of Jewish defence? Labour's understanding of Jewishness placed important political constraints on any defence it was likely to mount on behalf of this population. How could labour defend a population which had such an undesirable effect on the nation? Although the labour party itself, officially, issued no explicitly anti-semitic statements,[2] it did not exclude those who issued anti-semitic attacks from labour platforms.[3]

CONSTRAINTS

Labour's understanding of the political problems in East London, anti-semitism, and the manner in which they were addressed, were the product of specific conditions of emergence.[4] For labour, the central problem in East London was not anti-semitism, but fascism. Labour's anti-racism at this time was, in fact, a response to fascism. The interpretation that fascism was the problem to be addressed was constrained firstly by the style, actions and political focus of the British Union of Fascists (established in 1932) which emulated the symbolism, strategies and political concerns of their European counterparts. Detailed accounts of the British Union as a political force are provided by Skidelsky (1975), and Benewick (1969, 1972); it is here only of interest in so far as labour accorded it a central place in its political calculations. The British Union provided labour with a political target, and was seen as a central part of the problem to be addressed. It propounded a nationalism which demanded racial and financial purity, and a militarised style of politics which produced an aggressive form of anti-semitism.[5] Among its prominent theoreticians were Oswald Mosley, erstwhile labour theoretician and author of *Great Britain* (1932), Norman Leys and William Joyce. Despite its association with continental fascism, the British Union was a home-grown political product. Its leader, Oswald Mosley, had been politically reared in the Labour Party, where he developed what became a kind of corporatism, and which served as the basis of his approach to politics.[6] The British Union was also the political successor of the British Brothers' League, which was covertly anti-semitic (Nugent and King 1979: 32). Like

110

the British Brothers' League, the British Union was based in East London, and poorer parts of other major cities, where it was responsible for physical attacks on Jewish people and their property, most prevalent between 1934 and 1937.

The view that fascism was the key political problem of the 1930s was also sustained by labour's reading of events in Europe. This constitutes the second constraint producing labour's understanding of the political events in East London.[7] Labour focused on the rise of continental fascism, its relevance to Britain and the need for vigilance among the organised labour movement. Labour's focus was the impact of fascism on social democratic politics (Labour Party 1934, Joint Consultative Committee of the London Trades Council and the London Labour Party 1934, National Joint Council 1934b). This concern was produced by the dramatic collapse of the German Social Democratic Party, and subsequent treatment of communists, socialists and trade unionists in Germany, convincing labour that the actions of the British Union constituted an attack on the labour movement and its constituency, the working class.

The third constraint on labour's approach to the disturbances in East London was its anti-communism. To some extent labour shared its analysis of fascism with the Communist Party, and this drew labour once more into distinguishing itself from communism. Labour's opposition to the British Union, like its organisation of the trade union movement in India, was about asserting itself as a political agency, and a particular conception of socialism. Labour's struggle with the Communist Party was about who provided the best defence of the labour movement from fascism, and which were the appropriate political strategies to be deployed in this task. Labour's insistence on order and democracy, sustaining certain standards of political conduct, effectively constrained any defence it was able to offer the Jewish population of East London. The result of the constraints outlined, was that anti-semitic attacks in East London were officially seen as a problem of fascism, and its opposition. It is already apparent that anti-semitism was a marginal political concern for labour. This and its construction of Jewishness place some serious constraints on labour's ability to defend the Jewish population from racial attacks. This selection of political priorities and its implications become clearer as we look at labour's approach in more detail, and document some of the alternative conceptions available within the limits of labourism.

FASCISM

Labour's anti-racist strategy was constructed around its conception of the nature of the political problem it was addressing. Although the nature of a political problem and its resolution are intimately connected, we should not attempt to read off a strategy from the definition of a political problem, as the same problem can have many solutions, just as a single strategy can address any number of diverse political circumstances. Labour's understanding of the political problem in East London, which highlighted activities of the British Union as the perpetrators of British fascism, led it to focus on the British Union's rallies and street processions. Rallies were usually passionately anti-semitic, designed to inflame black-shirted audiences with racial hatred. Marches were commonly through Jewish districts and accompanied with racial taunts and destruction of Jewish property, as well as attacks on individual Jews, commonly referred to as 'Jew baiting' (*New Statesman and Nation* 3 November 1934: 615, 16 June 1934: 904–5, 10 October 1936: 496–7). British Union marches and rallies attracted opposition which often resulted in public disturbances. But for these street clashes between fascists and anti-fascists, it is unlikely that labour would have been involved in any form of opposition to anti-semitism. It was not labour's need to oppose anti-semitism which drew it into the political arena of East London, it was its need to contest the Communist Party's proffered defence of the working class from fascism, and assert a politics which insisted on public order.

Labour chose to define as fascism a problem which might have been defined as racism, for some of the reasons outlined in the discussion of constraints. There can be no doubt that physical attacks on populations defined using notions of racial difference, constitutes racism, in this case anti-semitism, and that this is a perfectly valid interpretation to place on events in East London at this time. Although the term racism was not used in the 1930s, labour had available and used the term racialism to describe the situation in East London. There were references to 'racial persecution' (Joint Consultative Committee of the London Trades Council and the London Labour Party 1934) 'racial strife' (Morrison 1936: 114), to 'anti-semitism' and 'racial hatred' (*Jewish Chronicle* 9 December 1938). Labour also accepted 'Jew baiting' as a description of events in East London (Poale Zion 1936). Certainly racialism was a key concept in this political discourse. Labour's focus on fascism accorded a subsidiary place to racism as a political problem. Racialism, for labour, was a political technique of fascism, and not the fundamental political problem to be addressed, which was fascism itself. Morrison (1936: 114) described racial strife as one of the 'provocative tactics of the fascists' along with civil disorder and a militarised style of politics. Racial strife in this context is obviously a reference to attacks on Jews, though neither Jewish people nor anti-semitism are directly mentioned in Morrison's NEC-sponsored, and hence authoritative, resolution at labour conference.

This official definition of the problem as fascism was a matter of consensus throughout the labour movement. Local labour parties focused on fascism (North East Bethnal Green Council May 1936), as did the key enunciative sites in the party: the Joint Consultative Committee of the London Trades Council and the London Labour Party (1934), the National Executive Committee (Morrison 1936), and the National Joint Council (1934b, 1934c, 1934d). Their analysis was repeated in conference speeches (Dukes 1934: 142), and shared by the Poale Zion (1935, 1936) and the Communist Party exhorting local East Enders to 'Stop Fascist Hooliganism in our Borough' (Bethnal Green Branch Communist Party undated, circa 1934–6).

Labour's prioritisation of fascism instead of racism has implications in terms of constituencies. Jews, who would have been the constituency of any struggle against racism, were marginalised by labour's focus on fascism. Given its construction of the significance of Jewishness in terms of a range of social pathologies, labour would have had difficulty in absorbing Jews as a constituency, or their political demands for defence as a priority. A concern with constituencies raises the question: Who was labour representing in offering fascism as a political target? Fascism was understood primarily as an attack on organised labour.

Congress draws the attention of the workers to the fact that wherever fascism has been instituted Trade Unionism,

Co-operation and Social-Democracy have been ruthlessly repressed and the standard of life of the workers has been degraded, personal and religious liberties and political freedom have been abolished, and methods of violence and savagery have dominated political and social life.

(Trades Union Congress 1934)

Fascism was an attack on all classes, but especially the working class, which, as its own constituency, labour was bound to defend (Morrison 1936). Jews could only be defended as part of the working class and not as a (racially demarcated) constituency in their own right. Still more about labour's priorities is revealed by deconstructing labour's conception of fascism, in order to see what was at stake in targeting it for political action.

DECONSTRUCTING FASCISM

What did fascism mean for labour? What was the constellation of political issues to which it refers? Racial strife, racialism and anti-semitism were part of fascism's field of concepts, revealed in the discourses surrounding labour's engagement in East London. But essentially fascism stood for three things requiring political opposition. Firstly, fascism stood for a way of organising a political community. It was a form of political organisation which was inferior to others, and specifically those organised with reference to democracy. Labour's analysis of continental fascism drew attention to its lack of freedom. In opposing fascism labour was defending order, progress and civilisation itself against the forces of totalitarianism, which included communism, and its unacceptable levels of political control over the individual (Labour Party 1933b). This represents a defence of that against which fascism was construed in labour discourse, democracy, and indicates that notions of democracy in fact organise labour's understanding of fascism. Fascism and democracy are related concepts in labour discourse. Democracy provided a standard of judgement against which totalitarianism could be specified, and subjected to critique. But fascism and democracy were also related discursive concepts in another sense. Fascism established itself in countries where democracy was weak (Joint Consultative Committee of the London Trades Council and the London Labour Party 1934: 1). Cracks in the edifice of democracy

114

provided the opportunity for fascism to establish itself. Avoiding this required the energetic defence of democracy. Democracy and fascism in labour discourse were interdependent political systems, and competing ways of organising the political community. The one defined and sustained the other.

Secondly, fascism and democracy did not just co-exist as political systems. Fascism was invasive of democracy as the erosion of workers' rights under fascist regimes on the continent had demonstrated (National Joint Council 1934d). In these formulations, workers and their political representatives were the guarantors of democracy. There were fears that the British Union, as well as attempting to turn Britain into a corporatist state, was also actively recruiting among the British working class.[8] The interpretation of fascism as an attack on workers was anxiously repeated, and provided a rallying point throughout the labour movement as the National Joint Council (1934b) resolution on fascism, to be presented at the annual conferences of the Labour Party and the Trades Union Congress, demonstrates. The very existence of fascism was an attack on the working class and the (democratic) system from which it had benefited. Labour represented that system, and the rights it had yielded for workers. The existence of fascism was, therefore, also an invasion of labourism. Labour's opposition to fascism was hence an act of self-defence.

Thirdly, fascism, in labour discourse, was a catalyst for social disorder. Social order is also the theme underlying labour's conceptions of fascism (as a mode of political organisation, and as an invasion of labourism) just explored, and the principle which unites all three conceptions. Public order was a key concept for labour, guiding its choice of political strategy. Labour chose to focus on the public order aspects of fascism, by highlighting fascist marches through Jewish areas such as the most famous march which became known in labour mythology as the Battle of Cable Street[9] (*Daily Herald* 5 October 1936), and by expressing its distaste of 'widespread disorder' whatever its cause (National Joint Council 1934c).[10] In addressing anti-semitic agitation, labour drew upon a framework establishing particular conceptions of socialism, and of itself as a political agency for anti-fascist (and not anti-racist) struggle.

But was labour's commitment to order and democracy

disabling of anti-racism? Did not order and democracy require the eradication of racial persecution and victimisation? Were not the attacks on Jewish residents of East London also an affront to public order? Despite evidence suggesting that the terrorisation of Jewish people in East London was extensive (Simon 1936: 1158), and that the forces of law and order were unable (or unwilling) to protect Jewish residents, a task which was falling to vigilante groups like the Association of Jewish Ex-Servicemen, labour did not see this form of racial attack as a public order issue. Although the forms of racial harassment suffered by Jews would have been every bit as disruptive as street clashes between fascist and anti-fascist forces, labour chose to overlook this, providing clear evidence that order and democracy were principles labour applied selectively. Labour did not defend Jewish people, though of course it disapproved of these attacks, even though Jewish defence could easily have been presented as a public order issue. It was not the case that labourism, at this time, could not support the demands made upon it, to defend constituencies defined with reference to racial difference. It chose not to.

Democracy for labour was more than a political principle. It was also a technique deployed around different political projects, evidence that claims on democracy can be made to sustain any political objective. Democracy was sometimes a technique for staking out a mode of political conduct not involving direct action and which defended, therefore (the existing) public order. In the case of anti-semitism, democracy was a technique used to curtail forms of political protest including street clashes. It was also a technique used to establish the superiority of Britain over other nations like India and the Soviet Union. Democracy was equated in a number of official publications[11] with higher forms of political development, reason and progress in the face of darkness and barbarism. Democracy was a technique used to challenge the Communist Party's leadership of the labour movement and socialism. Above all, democracy was a technique used to defend the Labour Party itself, from the Communist Party and from fascism. The underlying political project directing labour's deployment of democracy as a discursive technique, in the case of East London, was to assert and sustain itself as a political agency.

Labour's priorities were self-defence and not racial defence and this explains its approach to anti-semitism. Even the convergence of democracy and racial defence did not prompt labour to address anti-semitism directly. Jewish East Londoners were not just undefended in favour of other political priorities, they were indefensible. They were the focus for conflict, the civil disorder and the street clashes, which struck at the heart of labourism. Ultimately, in its East London struggles against fascism, labour was defending itself against the effects of the Jewish population on the political community. These principles were repeated much later in labour's dealings with multi-racialism and immigration in the 1960s as we have noted. Labour and Jews were antagonistic constituencies in political struggle, and this explains why Jews were not conceptualised as an object of racial persecution to be defended, even when their defence was perfectly consistent with a defence of public order and democracy.

Fascism was not the only available interpretation of events in East London. It was argued earlier that labourism also had available, within the Labour Party, concepts like racial and racialism as alternate definitions of the problem. The newly founded National Council for Civil Liberties (1936), for example, promised 'a vigorous campaign during the Autumn on these questions' of 'anti-semitic intimidation'. Likewise the *Jewish Chronicle* (9 September 1938: 21), focused on anti-semitism by publicising attacks on Jewish people. The *Jewish Chronicle* was a campaigning force working to convince the Board of Deputies of Anglo-Jewry[12] that anti-semitic attacks should be one of its concerns. This was something the Board avoided until 1936 on the grounds that its concern was Judaism. A definition of the problem in East London as primarily concerning racialism was most certainly available to the Labour Party in the 1930s. An analysis of racialism as a central and significant political problem would have marginalised fascism and the concerns which came with it: the prioritisation of labour as a political agency to be defended, and an understanding of Jewish people as part of the problem to be countered.

STRATEGY

Because labour was unable to define the problem in East London as racism, it is tempting to conclude that it becomes a nonsense to enquire further of its anti-racist strategy. Labour was incapable of an anti-racist strategy in the 1930s, because it chose not to define racism as a political problem. But in examining labour's opposition to fascism it becomes apparent that there were elements of an anti-racist strategy, in practice and at a local level. An examination of local labour responses to fascism in East London provides some valuable clues in piecing together the nature and limits of labourism, the relationship between local and national labour politics, and the force of political practice as a form of statement amenable to discourse analysis.

Notions of order, democracy and the need to assert itself as a political agency for socialism guided labour's official dealings with fascism. Labour's official anti-fascism comprised three strategies: political protest, propaganda campaigns involving public education, and judicial reform. Labour's approach to political protest was highly qualified by its need to avoid counter-demonstration and the disruption of fascist meetings: '. . . the organised Labour Movement repudiated entirely every form of organised interruption at public meetings' (National Joint Council 1934c). The condemnation of confrontational techniques, like the brawl between fascists and anti-fascists which arose from the disruption of the Olympia fascist rally in 1934, came from all major sites in the Labour Party, and was hence its official position.

> The attitude of the National Council for Labour was clearly defined in connection with the happenings at the Olympia meeting, when it was emphasized in the clearest and most emphatic terms that the organised Labour Movement repudiated entirely every form of organised interruption at public meetings. It need scarcely be pointed out that the proposal contained in the circular letter (urging the active disruption of fascist meetings) would almost inevitably lead to widespread disorder.
>
> (National Joint Council 1934c)

Above all political protest required the maintenance of public order, hence labour's support for defensive confrontation (Knowles 1979: 61–2). The public expression of a legitimate point of view at a political rally, organised to express opposition to fascism, was differentiated from demonstrations designed to prevent fascists marching through Jewish districts and from the disruption of fascist meetings. Labour's official opposition to fascism was, therefore, curtailed by a respect for order, and the right of the British Union to organise and express a political view, however abhorrent. This was later modified when labour joined the lobby for a public order bill, which became the Public Order Act (1936) and limited freedom of political expression. It was in defence of these principles of non-confrontation that labour warned the movement against turning out to oppose fascist marches through Jewish areas. 'Lansbury advises people to keep away from fascist demonstration in East End' (*Daily Herald* 1 October 1936: 1). Despite official disapproval, a counter-demonstration including many local party members blocked the passage of fascist marchers through a Jewish area, prompting widespread public disorder. 'Thousands of demonstrators barred the way when Sir Oswald Mosley and his Blackshirts attempted to march into the East End yesterday. . . . The crowds were aroused to fury by the Fascist's constant Jew baiting and marches into Jewish districts' (*Daily Herald* 5 October 1936: 1). A prominent labour voice, the *Daily Herald* tacitly approved this action despite National Executive condemnation (Morrison 1936), indicating a split in the labour movement.

Labour's official condemnation of confrontation was contested at all levels of party organisation, which mobilised to oppose fascism. The labour MP for Bethnal Green, for example, threatened to 'organise a force sufficiently powerful to deal with fascism' (Chater, undated, circa 1936). No less a local political figure than the Mayor of Bethnal Green, and the local Labour Party, met with Springhall Communist Party having arranged beforehand to meet and combine forces in a march on Cable Street to oppose the British Union's march (Springhall Communist Party 1 October 1936). This flouted two official policies, co-operation with the Communist Party, and attendance at counter-demonstrations, but such local activity was widespread between 1934 and 1937, and went unchallenged by party headquarters. This kind of support for confrontational strategies was not so much an enunciative challenge to the party, though there were challenges at conference on the politics of non-confrontation, as a decision to act on other considerations.

Eventually official policy shifted in 1936, when labour recognised that whilst it could not approve street confrontation, it could not expect its members to stand by and witness fascist provocation which should be circumscribed by law. Whilst this kind of direct confrontation may be seen as a defence against fascism, and not opposition to racism, it was a more direct involvement in Jewish defence than labour was prepared to entertain. The direct defence of Jewish people from the racial taunts of fascists was an important practical step in conceptualising attacks on Jews as racism.

Propaganda and education were central strategies in labour's official campaign against fascism. These were forms of political protest which did not require confrontation, and which respected order. The importance of literature exposing fascism and its objectives, preparing speaker's notes, party and trade union education to draw public attention to the 'dangers of fascism' (Joint Consultative Committee of the London Trades Council and the London Labour Party 1934), were important labour strategies, and demonstrate an awareness of the British Union's propaganda machine (Labour Party 1937c). In fact labour's pronouncements and education work on fascism were largely aimed at the labour movement itself. This provides further evidence that labour's priority was asserting and sustaining itself as a political agency, rather than opposing fascism, and that it feared fascism's appeal to the labour movement. The extent of fascism's hold on the labour movement was not something labour confronted openly.

Judicial reform was an important political strategy for labour in its dealings with fascism. Labour was divided over whether fascism, or more precisely its main political agency the British Union, was appropriately dealt with through public order legislation, or whether all political views were valid and defensible under the aegis of free speech. Initially labour officially supported free speech,[13] but this was successfully challenged following the street clashes of the autumn of 1936 which led to labour seeking audience with the Conservative Home Secretary to put the case for curtailing political expression through a public order act. The title of this act itself embodied a central labour priority. This debate about freedom of political expression split the Haldane Club (1935) which reported to the New Fabian

Research Bureau, in a bid to influence labour opinion. The majority decision of the Haldane Club and its labour oriented lawyers was to recommend against legislation 'since it would constitute an interference with personal liberty and would have the appearance of being a direct attack on a single political party'. A substantial minority, however, recommended the use of legislation to curtail the wearing of political uniforms as a means of political expression. Carefully defending the right of fascist to their views, it was proposed that legislation should simply curtail the use of militarism as a form of political expression. No mention was made of racial hatred, or physical attacks on Jews, which were clearly not intended as the objects of any proposed legislation.

The Public Order Act (1936), which was designed to prevent the wearing of political uniforms, exclude militarised political engagement, and ban demonstrations deemed likely to provoke public disorder, was officially supported by labour. In curtailing the 'wearing of uniforms in connection with political objects' the Public Order Act (Home Affairs Department 1936: 60) was unambiguously aimed at the activities of the British Union. It also allowed the banning of a certain 'class of public procession so specified' (Home Affairs Department 1936: 63). Reluctance on the part of the Home Secretary or police commissioners, who hold the power to ban demonstrations, to specify the content of 'class' has led, historically, to the act being used as a blanket-banning device to stop all processions. Once the act is invoked, even the Salvation Army cannot march without special permission. Labour missed the opportunity at the time when the Public Order Act became law to take a stand over the issue of 'classes' of public procession, and the content of militarised politics, by raising the issue of racial persecution, and incitement to racial hatred. Instead these were only tentatively raised thirty years later in the context of race relations legislation.

A UNITED FRONT AGAINST FASCISM

Questions of political strategy, agency and philosophy are all raised by labour's relationship to the United Front. The United Front was an anti-fascist alliance, created around the Socialist League, the Independent Labour Party and the Communist

121

Party[14] (National Joint Council 1934a). Labour's response to the United Front indicates much about the nature of labourism, highlighting some of the central issues raised in this chapter, notably labour's insistence on a dominant role for itself in any struggle against fascism, to be achieved by challenging the Communist Party. The basis on which the Communist Party was challenged for the leadership of the labour movement draws upon notions of order and democracy, and ties together some of the major themes raised in this chapter.

The United Front became a major issue for labour. In terms of labour's statement output, the United Front was more significant than the political forces it was designed to counter. Statements from central enunciative sites in the party warned of the dangers of communism, internationally and in Britain, including related organisations such as the Relief Committee for the Victims of German Fascism.[15] (Labour Party 1933b, undated circa 1937a, 1937b, 1937c). Labour's objections to the Relief Committee show that the opposition of fascism was secondary to opposition to communism. East London was the site of a battle between the Labour Party and the Communist Party, about which was the real force for socialism and the best political agency to represent the working class. The following statement captures many of the features of this struggle.

> Dictatorship [in Europe] has usurped the place of democracy. Elected representatives have been imprisoned by triumphant reaction. . . . Religious and racial intolerance in its vilest forms has reappeared. Masses of the working class electors – divided between communism and social democracy – have fallen victims to Fascism. . . . British labour has led the world in its claim for industrial democracy and its demand for political democracy. Its historic task today is to uphold the principles of social democracy . . . its fundamental faith.
>
> (National Joint Council 1933b)

The title of the document from which this statement was taken, 'Democracy Versus Dictatorship', sums up labour's approach to the United Front. Herbert Morrison (1933: 219), in introducing this document at labour conference, explains the impossibility of co-operating with the Communist Party 'because they themselves believe in a form of dictatorship . . . we condemn dictatorship as such, whether that dictatorship is a dictatorship of the Left or of the Right'. In support of this analysis, and following the events of Cable Street, the *Daily Herald* quoted with approval a similar view expressed by the Secretary of State for War, Duff-Cooper (15 October 1936: 2) denouncing the clashes in East London as clashes 'Between the supporters of two foreign creeds . . . the majority of Englishmen have no sympathy with red Communism or black Fascism, and we resent it deeply that the supporters of alien doctrines should make our city hideous'. Totalitarianism was not only an affront to democracy, it was un-English, like the Jews whose presence provoked this battle of foreign creeds. 'Democracy Versus Dictatorship' was controversial, and fiercely contested at the 1933 party conference, providing evidence of divergence in labour approaches on this, as on other issues.[16]

CONCLUSION

In the 1930s racism was not a political problem in its own right. Although labour had a conception of racialism, this at best designated the defence of Jews, a secondary political issue to fascism. Despite having a notion of racialism, labour had no conception of anti-racism. Labour's dominant conception of fascism was a defence of public order and democracy, and the legitimate representative of these principles: itself. Far from conceptualising Jewish people as a constituency to be defended, they were officially regarded as part of the problem, because they provided a focus for fascist and anti-fascist agitation. The unofficial defence of the Jewish population involved in counter-demonstration, was as close as labour came to defending Jewish people. The limits of labourism, if not official labourism, at least sustained this kind of political initiative. Unable to challenge racism, labour did manage to present something of a challenge to fascism. But even in its strategies designed to challenge fascism, labour was limited by its notions of political order and its need to challenge the Communist Party, in asserting itself as the real leader of working class struggle. Labour's major focus was to assert and sustain itself as a political agency. It was, in the 1930s, unable to countenance any form of anti-racist struggle, despite having a conception of public order, which could have supported a limited defence of Jews from racial attack. These are the historical roots of labour's anti-racism, and provide the conditions of emergence of its defence of Britain's black population in the mid-1970s, in similar circumstances.

8

ANTI-RACISM IN THE 1970s

This chapter addresses a number of key issues. What was labour's understanding of racism? And what were the political strategies through which it was addressed? What did labour's anti-racism consist of in the 1970s? What were the conditions of emergence of racism and anti-racism as significant concepts for labour in this period? Are there any ways in which these are informed by labour's dealings with anti-racism in the 1930s? This chapter, like the last, is concerned to establish labour's credentials as a force for anti-racist struggle. This chapter deals with some of the political events which occurred between 1976 and 1979, and which raised racism as a political concern for labour. Opposition to racism emerged on labour's political agenda in 1976 with the announcement of major campaigns by the National Executive Committee, and by the Trades Union Congress (Labour Party 1977: 308). There was also more extensive coverage given to anti-racism in *Labour Weekly* (30 July 1976: 5, 20 August 1976: 5) signalling its significance as an issue. Racism was produced as a particular kind of issue for labour in the 1970s. It was the product of some significant constraints, providing its conditions of emergence.

RACE POLITICS IN THE 1970s

A number of factors in race politics converged in the mid-1970s, structuring labour's approach to racism, forming its conditions of emergence. The mid-1970s was a period when race politics was running out of legislative initiative. The patriality of the 1971 Immigration Act had ensured that immigration was reduced to a

125

trickle of dependants, and the third of three attempts to provide a legal framework for multi-racialism, in the form of the 1976 Race Relations Act, was about to be put in place. This converged with a particular conjunction of circumstances in local urban politics. The Labour government's cuts in public expenditure had hit town halls, jeopardising inner city funding designed to alleviate what Labour saw as the urban stress imposed by black populations, on the living standards of the white working class. Solomos (1989: 90) argues that the 1960s measures designed to alleviate urban stress, the Local Government Act (1966) and the Local Government Grants (Special Needs) Act (1969) had a limited impact anyway on race policy development in local authorities. Local cuts which imposed severe constraints on urban life caused protest around the services they attacked. The latter half of the 1970s also saw urban disturbances in London, Birmingham and Liverpool, sparked by insensitive policing in black areas. The campaign to have what were popularly known as the 'sus laws', which allowed the wholesale harassment of black people under the 1824 Vagrancy Act on the grounds that they were suspected of having committed, or being about to commit a crime, removed was mounting. Black urban unrest was slow to feed into local politics despite Section 71 of the 1976 Race Relations Act which required local authorities to promote equal opportunity (Solomos 1989: 92). Ouseley (1990: 132) argues that race equality initiatives were only just appearing on local political agendas. These were to become significant in structuring labour race politics in the 1980s.

Labour had also constructed, from the late 1950s, a particular significance for blackness through its dealings with race relations, urban funding and immigration policies. It was noted in chapters five and six that labour's understanding of blackness associated it with disorder, violence and a matrix of social problems focusing on the inner city, and the conflictual relationships between racially distinguished populations. Black immigrants were construed by labour as a distinctive and oppositional political community, whose distinctiveness consisted of stresses placed on the host community. Characterised as the bearers of lower health standards, lower educational standards and lower standards of political association, black immigrants were bound to be a focus for a defensiveness about

126

the character of the political community itself. Labour had itself constructed blacks and whites as oppositional political communities, through its construction of indigenousness and exteriority in its postwar engagement with race issues. Given their location in labour discourse, what kind of defence of Britain's black population would labour offer?

Racism became an issue for labour through the campaigns of the National Front. The National Front, formed in 1967, was the largest and most popular in a group of nationalistic political forces demanding racial purity through repatriation (Taylor 1979: 124, Nugent and King 1979: 37).[1] Adopting the imagery of nazism in its political style and symbolism, and subsuming anti-semitism beneath an explicit campaign of violence and harassment directed at Britain's black population, the thug-image of the National Front was developed through political rallies and marches through black areas. It was this particular form of racism that catalysed the Labour Party into anti-racist action. The parallels between the activities of the National Front and the British Union were striking, and labour relied on past formulations in developing its opposition to this particular form of politics. But for the National Front, labour may not have taken an anti-racist stand. The National Front ensured that labour responded, but response was severely constrained by the political agenda set by the Front, and the manner in which labour had responded to this style of politics in the 1930s. As in the 1930s, labour was reactive and defensive in its anti-racism.

SOCIAL JUSTICE

Labourist conceptions of racism at this time, defining the nature of the problem to be addressed by anti-racist action, have as their general framework the creation of a fairer society, and focus on a number of concerns. The first of these concerns locates racism in terms of systems of economic and social distribution. The effects of social distribution meant that 'In general blacks are in the worst jobs, have lower earnings and occupy the poorest housing – often in inner city areas' (Labour Party 1979: 1).[2] This signals a growing recognition that access and distribution were at the root of racism, and a shift in labour thinking towards conceptualising social distribution as an effect produced by a racist society, and not an index of black capacity. Racism as a feature of social distribution incorporated black people into a familiar labour constituency, the poor, highlighting simultaneously levels of black wages. Wages were, of course, a familiar labour and trade union concern, though in the past, black immigrant and white indigenous wages had been placed in competition with each other. A concern with black wages prompted the appearance of labour and trade union leaders on the Grunwick picket lines in 1977, offering for the first time backing for a dispute involving black workers (and in which women played a prominent part) from the commanding heights of the labour movement (Miles and Phizacklea 1979a: 104). The Grunwick dispute, like the National Front, made racism a labour issue. Both captured the interest of local constituency parties, in a way which other race issues, like opposition to immigration for example, had not (Hendon South Constituency Labour Party 14 December 1977: 1). Concern over social distribution gave labour a point of access to racism, as it raised familiar concerns and constituencies in labourist politics. Racism in this sense also provided labour the opportunity to assert a political leadership over a poor black working class, a claim which labour was to develop in a particular way in the 1980s. Labour's conceptualisation of racism as a matter of social distribution was important in shifting labour race politics in the 1970s, and in leading labour to claim a black constituency it had previously differentiated in terms of social pathology.

Secondly, allied to social distributions, were social conditions, and their part in generating racial hostility. Social conditions accounts of racism require a theory of ideology, and see racism as a system of beliefs fed by the social disadvantages of a host community, who, in competition over scarce resources, displace their hostility onto black populations. This working class racism thesis was in line with academic output in the 1970s, which examined concerns also expressed at the level of political action, that the working class was predisposed to the politics of the National Front, and needed to be reclaimed for struggles around social justice (Miles and Phizacklea 1979a: 104). In taking on social conditions conceptions of racism, labour was involving itself in consideration of the nature and forms of racial prejudice, the conditions which generate and sustain it, and the extent to which this had penetrated labour's constituency, the working class. Never before had racism been given such detailed attention by labour.

Contributors to this social conditions theory were high unemployment, declining living standards and public expenditure cuts which 'breed[s] racism' (Labour Party 1979: 46) or 'which racialists use to stimulate racial prejudice' (Labour Party 1979: 1). Social conditions affecting the deprivation of blacks and whites in the inner cities produced 'real grievances' among the population, which were diverted onto 'racial minorities' (Labour Party 1979: 49). The idea that adverse social conditions produced racism was labour's official policy (National Executive Committee 1978: 1), and was widely supported throughout the labour movement (Murray and Keys 1978: 63, Cope 1977: 309). 'But Governments must recognise that unemployment and urban deprivation feed the seeds from which racialism can grow. Short-term economic measures can cause long term social problems for all of us' (Lestor 15 October 1976). Racism as a set of hostile prejudices was prompted by high unemployment, causing racial tension, and allowing the 'scapegoating tactics of the fascists' (Labour Party 1979: 46, 49, Carless 1977: 311). This association between racism and the demand for full employment made it possible to claim that 'the eradication of racial discrimination is an integral part of the ongoing struggle for socialism' (Garland 1977: 309). Social conditions, like social distribution, allowed the incorporation of racism into the framework of a labourist politics. This was something which could have happened in the 1930s, but did not because of the significances attached to racial difference by labour. Racism as an ideology was activated by the National Front, which was presented as an agency for racist agitation. This link between racism and its political agency provided the convergence of labour's concern with fascism, and its concern for social conditions. The National Front provided a target which addressed, though to a limited extent, these political concerns. The National Front thus activated some old labour responses, and provided a focus for some new ones, or at least concerns which were newly applied to black populations.

The incorporation of a struggle against racism into labourist politics must be set against another tendency in labourist

129

discourse. The influence of racism on the political forces struggling for socialism, the working class, was now an issue for comment and concern. There were acknowledgements from official sources that the National Front was attracting workers' votes (Labour Party 1979: 70–1). A statement from Bethnal Green and Stepney Trades Council (1978: 30) referring to a paper written by a trade unionist on racism in trade unions, claims that the author of this paper explored a taboo subject when 'He faces the harsh reality that racialist sentiment is already deeply rooted in the working class'. Similar concerns about the political affiliations of the working class, and their political representatives, were also evident in a circular from the Trades Union Congress to affiliated unions, warning that known racialists and fascists on trades councils would not be tolerated (Murray and Keys 1978: 63). Recognition that the labour and trade union movement itself sustained racist beliefs, is scattered throughout the records of this period.[3] This was a significant development for labour from its 1930s position. In the 1930s labour ignored expressions of racism from within its own ranks, or obliquely addressed its propaganda against fascism to the labour movement itself, without openly admitting that racist hostility was a persuasive force among labour's constituency. What remains unacknowledged is the part played by the Labour Party itself in construing a different kind of racial hostility, generated around its construction of multi-racialism in the 1960s and early 1970s. In responding to racism in the labour movement, labour was addressing some of the damage it had been instrumental in creating in the first place.

FASCISM

The key political agency and active force making a link between poor social conditions, and their ideological effects in the working class, was the National Front. The significance of the National Front is that it forms the third of labour's concerns in locating an understanding of racism, and provided a dominant image for racism throughout the labour movement. The National Front became a symbol of racism in the 1970s, and hence itself a force to be countered. It became the problem, and succeeded in mobilising the labour and trade union movement against racism in a way which might not otherwise have occurred. What precisely did the National Front stand for in labour's political calculations? What was the link between fascism and racial hostility? Was it the case that labour's assault on fascism was also, like it was in the 1930s, an act of self-defence?

Fascism and racism were, as in the 1930s, related concepts in a discourse on race. Fascism, and not racialism, had dominated the discourse in the 1930s, but by the 1970s these two concepts were used interchangeably, indicating that they referred to the same range of political problems.[4] This was certainly the case in key official statements (Murray and Keys 1978: 63, Labour Party 1979) and there is no evidence that these were subjected to any major enunciative challenge. Labour's conception of fascism in the late 1970s was clearly influenced by the frameworks it had constructed in the 1930s, set out at length in *Race, Immigration and the Racialists* (Labour Party 1979). Fascism for labour was both invasive of the working class, at one time referred to as 'a crawling loathsome mental disease' (Whine 1948: 181), and an international political force recalling 1930s European links (Bethnal Green and Stepney Trades Council 1978: 39). Fascism was accorded the historic associations with nazism it claimed for itself as a set of representative images (Labour Party 1979: 77, Adams 1978: 312). This was captured by the popular slogan of the time 'The National Front is a Nazi Front' (Trades Union Congress and the Labour Party, undated, circa 1978, Lerner 1976: 214).

Nationalism was also an important feature of fascism for labour, and this provided an obvious link with racism. Distinguishing finance from productive capital, and national from international capital, the National Front, like the British Union before it, provided both a basis for British nationalism and an appeal to a greater diversity of class interests than labour itself (Labour Party 1979: 72). This nationalism included a demand for racial purity which, by the 1970s, was implicitly anti-semitic (substituting the term Jew with references to Zionism and internationalism) and explicitly anti-black, in its demand for the repatriation of black Britons (Labour Party 1979: 73, 76). The link between anti-semitism and anti-black racism was made by labour in a reference to Hitler's repatriation schemes on the road to the concentration camps and gas chambers (Labour Party

1979: 77). This reference also establishes anti-black racism, like anti-semitism, as a product of fascism. This link was, in fact, established in a 1948 conference resolution on 'Racial discrimination and fascist activities', which repeated labour's classic 1930s formulation of fascism and its (racially distinguished) victims, to which was added concern over the 'colour bar' and the banning of 'negroes' from British sports and restaurants (Smith 1948: 181). Fascism offered a context for anti-black racism as well as anti-semitism, providing an important link with the 1930s, and a set of ready-formulated political responses.[5]

Fascism in 1970s labour discourse, like in the 1930s, required the 'complete destruction of democratic process' in its authoritarian style of government, and control of the press (Labour Party 1979: 70, 75). Hence the labour and trade union movement itself was still the main object of fascism's attacks, and fascism's real motive was the erosion of workers' rights (Labour Party 1979: 73–5, Adams 1978: 312). This claim was still underscored by references to fascism in Germany and Italy and its 1930s attacks on social democratic parties and trade unions in a search for a corporate state. This compares the foreignness of fascism, and its opposition to democratic process, to the 'socialism and christianity' for which labour stood (Labour Party 1979: 70). Populations designated with reference to racial characteristics were still the first in a line of victims, ultimately converging on democracy itself. 'Yesterday it was the Jews. Today it is coloured Britons. Tomorrow it could be trade unionists' (Trades Union Congress and the Labour Party, undated, circa 1978). Anti-racists were victims too. 'The major focus of the venom of right wing extremists has been against the white anti-racists as much as against the immigrant community' (Bethnal Green and Stepney Trades Council 1978: 38). Anti-racism was once more an act of self-defence by the labour movement. Racial violence and attack were some of the tactics of fascism, and the link between fascism and racism remained as it was in the 1930s. Black Britons, like Jews, could not be a priority constituency for labour; their defence was incorporated in a defence of democracy. Fascism offered a context for racism, and this is the nature of the link between the two concepts. Increasingly, references to fascism fade, and racism becomes the commonly used term referring to a multiplicity of forms of racial disadvantage.

As well as providing a familiar context for racism, making it a labour issue, fascism also provided the labour movement with a focus for political mobilisation. Fascism mobilised local constituency parties like no other issue (Hendon South Constituency Labour Party 5 May 1977: 2, 14 December 1977: 3, 12 August 1977: 2).[6] It also spawned anti-racist committees throughout the country, around local labour politics. Local defence committees were set up in response to racist attacks, and the Anti-Nazi League arose out of the need to provide a street presence to contest the National Front (Messina 1989: 119). The capacity of the National Front for mobilising the labour movement indicates the extent to which the political analysis which offered fascism as a key target for anti-racists held throughout the labour movement.[7]

The concerns so far described, social conditions, social distribution and a racial hostility mobilised by fascist forces, formed a clustering of concepts around racism in the 1970s. They draw upon concerns of the 1930s, but also effect some important shifts. The 1970s saw a re-alignment in labour race politics, and the basis for some new possibilities around anti-racism, rooted in some old approaches. Within this consensual clustering offered by social conditions and so on, there was an important political divergence affecting the ordering of political priorities. A significant axis of divergence in anti-racist politics at this time concerned whether the National Front itself, or the racial violence with which it was associated, was the more significant political target. Whilst both of these positions shared an analysis of racism, they diverge over the question of emphasis and constituencies. Anti-racist politics organised around racial attacks (offering a racial violence focus) were popular locally, and offered black Britons as a priority constituency. An example of this form of politics was set out in the Bethnal Green and Stepney Trades council publication *Blood on the Streets* (1978) and may be seen as a bid to define labour's race politics priorities towards constituencies defined with reference to racial difference. The politics this was opposing, a politics centrally concerned with fascism as a political target (offering a public order and incitement to racial hatred focus), took on racism as a side-issue to the defence of the labour movement (and hence the working class) as a whole, though in doing so it became transformed. This was labour's official approach to racism, and was challenged by concerns with racial violence in local labour politics. The assertion of racial violence, and hence black defence, as a significant political target provided an important watershed in labour race politics.

RACIAL VIOLENCE

Analyses of racism which focused on racial violence stressed levels of physical attack on Britain's black community, coupled with concerns about ineffective policing. These were a bid to redefine racism contesting in small, but significant respects, official concerns with public order and incitement. The analysis offered by Bethnal Green and Stepney Trades Council (1978) emerged around the establishment of a local anti-racist committee, as in other urban areas with black populations suffering attack, and is indicative of a form of politics which had a significant local following. Their analysis of racism provides an insight into local labour race politics. It documents the serious extent of racial attacks in this part of London, recording 119 racially motivated attacks between 1976 and 1978, and the murders of Ishaque Ali and Altab Ali (1978).[8] This was coupled with a demand that the labour government investigate and act upon the complaints of the local Bengali population. This example of a challenge to official policy demonstrates how local labour concerns differ from official, centrally organised policy, and how local concerns can feed into central processes. The form of politics asserted by the Bethnal Green Trades Council were taken up, and formed an important enunciative challenge to the party at conferences in the late 1970s, where it focused attention on whether the state, or vigilante groups, were going to defend black populations (Bidwell 1977: 314, Adams 1978: 313). Although this approach to racism did not gain official sanction, it was an effective force in shifting official policy, as an examination of labour's approach to public order reveals. This local challenge to official labourism was effective because it shared a conceptual clustering organised by the concept racism. It shared the official view that the National Front was a significant force to be countered (as the perpetrators of racial abuse) and exploited labour's concern with public order, using it to provide a link with racial violence.

Other enunciative challenges to official policy definitions of racism include concerns that policing was a significant contributor to racism. There was a good deal of concern at this time that the police not only failed to protect black people from racial attacks, but the police themselves were responsible for racial harassment, in the levels and manner of policing offered in black areas. The use of the 'sus' laws (eventually repealed) on black youth and the raiding and surveillance of black communities, were important concerns existing within the limits of labourism, but which did not direct official action (Adams 1978: 312). Enunciative challenges like this one were often linked to criticism of labour's immigration policy (Adams 1978: 312). This was later taken more seriously in the 1980s as labour publicly regretted its stance on immigration and pledged itself to reform. The 1970s provided some important challenges to labour race politics which were later to find their way into official policy. The policy review exercise still commits labour to examining police–black relations and to the provision of non-discriminatory immigration controls.

PUBLIC ORDER AND INCITEMENT TO RACIAL HATRED

Officially, labour was concerned to define racism in terms of public order. Concerns about public order were still a high priority for labour in the 1970s, and there can be no doubt that the problems presented by the National Front were seen in this context. In the conviction that 'public order and racialism are indissolubly linked', Labour's National Executive Committee (1978: 2) announced its intention to deal with racism using public order legislation. Officially, racism was a problem of the public, disruptive activities of the fascist National Front. In focusing on public order, labour was offering a highly restricted approach to a narrowly defined problem. Re-activating a 1930s framework, successive labour Home Secretaries pressed on the labour movement the 'need to avoid creating unnecessary physical confrontations which only play into the hands of media-conscious bigots' (Rees 19 November 1976). A similar position was set out by Merlyn Rees's predecessor in outlining an approach for anti-racists – 'it is the persuasion of their arguments rather than their physical presence on the streets which is desirable' (Jenkins 30 July 1976: 7). Concern with public order relegates the content of a racist politics to a secondary position, and with it the constituency forming its object of attack, black Britons. Labour's priority was firstly to assert the requirement for a certain style of political conduct for the community in the organisation of political protest; and secondly to represent the labour movement as a priority constituency in a struggle against fascism. Black populations, like Jews in the 1930s, were only to be defended in this context, and not as a priority constituency in their own right.

It was noted in the context of the 1930s, that public order was a political priority capable of sustaining the defence of populations suffering racial attack. Labour eventually acknowledged that public order required the defence of black communities, under the influence of local concerns about racial violence. Marking a significant transition point in labour race politics, labour established an official, stated concern about the security of black Britons.

> The Home Secretary and I [Merlyn Rees] are very much concerned about the incidence of crimes of violence in the East End of London and about the fears of the Bangladeshi community. The activities of those who give rise to these fears are to be deplored . . . [and we promise to] increase the number of police posted there in the longer term.
>
> (Home Office 1978: 91–2)

But it was a labour government which failed to direct the effective policing of black areas. Because labour did not implement its concern, black populations remained effectively a secondary political constituency. Here is an obvious disjuncture between different levels of discourse, between statement and action. But an important principle had been established in labour making this declaration.

Labour's acknowledgement of black defence as a significant political priority was part of a process which saw the emergence of a broader approach to racism. This broke the 1930s mould of labour race politics, providing further evidence that the 1970s were a period of political re-alignment. Out of labour's concern for public order grew the recognition that 'racialism is not merely an issue of public order' (National Executive Committee 1978: 4). The nature of fascism itself and particularly racial hatred and violence, emerged as a significant dimension of racism. By 1978 labour was looking for a legal framework to curb the activities of the National Front, but one which would deal with racial hatred, and not just public order (Labour Party 1979: 46, Rees 1977: 312–13). By 1978, labour was looking for a way to ban marches likely to cause 'racial hostility or prejudice towards any racial group' (National Executive Committee 1978: 4). This was an important statement of political principle, a direct reference to race, and not a blanket defence of public order (whatever the principle) as in the 1930s. This represents a recognition by labour that racism (in the form of racial hostility) could be a political priority, and with it the defence of a constituency designated with reference to racial characteristics.

This was a breakthrough in labour race politics. The tension between race and class politics in the 1930s broke, and revealed the possibility of race as a political concern. Labour had, historically, used public order as a framework for race politics. In the 1930s, racially defined populations could only be conceptualised as requiring a disciplinarity, whether in India or in Britain, as in the case of the Jews. This position was only slowly changing in the 1960s, when race relations legislation prioritised the conduct of the political community, over a defence of black people from discrimination. In the late 1970s we see the emergence of the idea that black people had rights, which should be defended, and that these could form political priorities in their own right without recourse to a more general defence of the working class. The establishment of race as a political priority in the debates over incitement and racial violence in the 1970s mark the important feature of the re-alignment taking place in race politics, placing race in a new position on labour's political agenda.

The tension between race and class in terms of political priorities and constituencies represents two important strands of labour thinking both, from the late 1970s, capable of attracting official support. Race politics, once relegated to the boundaries of labourism, has found some influence with central enunciative sites in the party. But its hold remains tenuous and the tension remains. The labour movement slogan of the late 1970s 'Black and white unite and fight' represents an analysis which still asserts the primacy of class struggle, its political objectives and constituencies, in which black Britons are invited to take their chances in the lottery of social justice in the same way as the rest of the working class. Official recognition that the working class was not homogenous, but dissected by significant social divisions such as race, marked an important step for labour. These tension points between race and class, which in practical political intervention require the ordering of political priorities, are still played out in the debates over Labour Party black sections, discussed in the next chapter.

POLITICAL STRATEGY

Labour's political strategies for dealing with anti-racism in the 1970s were clearly informed by its dealings with anti-semitism in the 1930s, but also involve some significant departures. A key, official strategy for labour was still the use of legislation, this time to circumscribe the activities of the National Front (Rees 1977: 312–13). This was a strategy attracting support from the membership of the party too (Hawkins 1977: 310). Although labour did still operate a public order framework relying on the 1936 Public Order Act, it now required legislation to deal specifically with public expressions of racial hostility, and for this it looked to the strengthening of the 1976 Race Relations Act (National Executive Committee 1978: 4). Although labour was still using legislation, it was using it in a different way. It was using it to defend the principle that public expressions of racial hostility were unacceptable, and not just to insist on public order. Public order was still important to labour, but it was now mediated by other concerns.

Propaganda and education remained a significant official strategy, familiar from the 1930s, and still aimed at labour's own membership (Rees 19 November 1976: 5, Labour Party 1979: 46). Much of this consisted of warnings about the dangers of the National Front, but some took up the issue of immigration and dealt with some of the popular myths surrounding it. This provides evidence that labour's membership itself still required convincing that immigrants were not pouring into Britain. Marches and demonstrations were also significant official strategies (Labour Party 1979: 48). Protest was to take place within the same limits as in the 1930s, a view which had some influence in the constituencies; 'the answer is not violent confrontation with the National Front' (Hawkins 1977: 311). As in the 1930s this was not a matter of consensus in the party. There were those who favoured mass demonstration and violent confrontation.

> The labour movement – the mass of the trade unions and the Labour Party – have not mobilised. I say that when fascists mobilise, the mass power of trade unions and of the labour movement must be mobilised against them. We must have thousands to mobilise against them.
>
> (Knights 1977: 313)

Labour's official commitment to the defence of the black community taking place in local labour politics, as it did in the 1930s, was circumscribed by its historical commitment to certain standards of political conduct.

Labour's official strategy of inner city funding as an assault on social deprivation was a departure from the 1930s.[9] Although the association of race with urban deprivation was a 1930s theme, labour was uneasy about multi-racialism, rather than prepared to deal with it through enhanced funding. Another significant departure from the 1930s was labour's tacit support for (or at least its toleration of) the proliferation of organisations which appeared specifically to deal with racism. These organisations were quite varied. There was the carnival approach of the Anti-Nazi League, formed in 1977 to mobilise the young and unorganised in the cause of anti-racism, and providing anti-racism with an up-beat image. As the title of this organisation conveys, though, it favoured the old official labour party analysis that fascism was the main problem. The Anti-Nazi League was a force for extra-parliamentary action and rapidly developed a large organisational structure capable of mobilising thousands in counter-demonstrations against the National Front (Messina 1989: 118). Mass action and counter-demonstration did not isolate the Anti-Nazi League from the Labour Party, though the league was not officially endorsed.[10] There were also defence committees, set up to address the issue of racial violence and which operated around local labour politics. The Hackney and Tower Hamlets Defence Committee in London, for example, was set up as part of a mobilisation which came out of a meeting called by the local Community Relations Council, attended by representatives of twenty-six ethnic minority and anti-racist groups. This was a form of political organisation involving black groups, and emerged as a response to the murder of Isaque Ali (Bethnal Green and Stepney Trades Council 1978: 55). Hackney and Tower Hamlets' 'black solidarity day' (1978), in protesting against racist violence, closed sections of the Ford Body plant in their mobilisation of trade unionists against racial violence (Bethnal Green and Stepney Trades Council 1978: 58). Anti-racism was gaining support throughout the labour and trade union movement. Mobilisation was occurring around racism and in local single issue campaigns, and not, as in the 1930s, around an opposition to fascism.

CONCLUSION

It has been argued in this chapter that the latter half of the 1970s saw some significant re-alignments in labour race politics. Labour dealt with racism by incorporating it into labourism. It did this by constructing racism in terms of social distribution, social conditions and the mobilisation of racial hostility by the National Front. In this way anti-racism became part of a general demand for social justice, which had to be extended to include black Britons. This conception of racism re-activated some of the concerns of the 1930s, significantly restructuring them. Gradually fascism was replaced by a concern for racism, which was seen as a political issue requiring its own solutions. This challenge to official labourism occurred around local labour politics, and was organised around the demand for the defence of the black community from racial violence, a demand which significantly included black voices. The tension between class and race politics came to a head with the official recognition that racial hatred and hostility were an important aspect of racism, and required their own political strategies. Black Britons became a labour constituency around their requirement for defence from race hatred. This replaced the analysis of the 1930s, still evident in the 1960s, that black Britons were a distinctive political community from which an indigenous community needed to be defended. Although recognition of the significance of racial hostility still constructs black populations in terms which locate them as an object of racial hostility, this was now coupled with an insistence that this be countered as a political priority, and not as part of a general defence of the working class. The late 1970s was an important transition point in the construction of the social significance of blackness in labour discourse. This transition occurred around a construction of anti-racism and its associated political strategies. The multi-racial community was accepted as a permanent feature of a plural society. Black Britons had made the transition from being a separately construed community, to being a potential labour constituency, a process which would continue and take a particular political direction in the 1980s.

9

BLACK REPRESENTATION
Prospects for the 1990s

Labour race politics in the 1980s produced some further shifts
and re-alignments. These are the result of two sources of
pressure, attempting to reformulate labour politics in the
direction of racial equality. The proliferation of race equality
concerns at the municipal level, over the delivery of services to
local black populations, has had an important impact on the
Labour Party centrally. So too has labour's attempted to develop
its relationship with a black constituency, in declaring its
intention to build a multi-racial party. These two pressures, one
central and one local, have placed the issue of black
representation on labour's political agenda. Any political party
offering itself as a force in anti-racist politics must inevitably
confront its relationship with those whose political aspirations
and demands it claims to represent. Black involvement does not
in itself guarantee that labour will develop effective policies to
deal with racism. But an agency challenging racism which does
not incorporate the demands of black Britons will obviously be
limited. A construction of an anti-racist politics which excludes
black voices is unlikely to be effective, either in defining the
issues to be addressed, or in mobilising the political will to
address them. The issue of black representation has dominated
labour race politics since 1983, and remains unresolved.

The Labour Party, with its conception of social justice, is
capable of sustaining a demand for racial equality. Reconstructed
socialism, as it emerged from the policy review (see Labour Party
1988, 1989), provides a conception of citizenship which could
easily be applied to black citizens. The only question is – is it
prepared to do so? The Labour Party provides the only hope that

anti-racism will enter mainstream British politics, and address the concerns of black Britons. Labour's handling of black representation is therefore a vitally important issue. At the heart of this issue are some important concerns regarding the nature of the Labour Party as a political agency, and its potential for developing an anti-racist politics for the 1990s. This chapter examines labour's handling of the demand for black representation. It reveals some of the important stumbling blocks for labour in creating a multi-racial party. The demand for black representation requires some reforms in the Labour Party including a preparedness to sustain forms of politics which centrally concern race struggles. Labour made an important start in this direction in the 1970s, but this form of politics is constantly contested by other concerns which focus on class politics. Labour's handling of black representation reveals its limitations as a political agency, and the gap between statement and political action, as forms of discourse.

CONDITIONS OF EMERGENCE OF RACE POLITICS TODAY

Labour's race politics in the 1990s are the product of three general constraints. These generated the political space for the re-alignments which have occurred: its conditions of emergence. Restructuring, disciplinarity and recognition of the significance of a black constituency, are conditions peculiar to the 1980s. They combine with the conditions created by the re-alignments of the mid-1970s, to make labour's race politics what they are today.

The restructuring of labourism through the policy review in the 1980s, in an attempt to up-date labour's conception of socialism and make it electable, provided the opportunity for making the party more sensitive to racial inequality. It was noted in chapter two that reconstructed socialism has incorporated some important gains for a feminist politics, decades after the establishment of the women's section of the party. The existence of the women's section is obviously important in supporting the demand for black section representation. The women's section also provides an important lesson in how long it has taken women, despite having their own organisation in the party, to achieve so little from labour. Labour has allowed the restructuring of socialism to provide gains around an equal opportunity politics, but which pay only minimal attention to racial equality. This is a matter of deliberate exclusion, as socialism for the 1990s is capable of sustaining a demand for racial equality through a notion of citizenship rights (see chapter two). The status of the policy review, and whether it will ever find an expression in practice, remains to be seen, but this deliberate exclusion of black demands in the party provides some important clues about contemporary labourism. Despite acknowledgement in the 1970s that socialism required racial equality, labour still has difficulty incorporating racial equality into socialism which retains its trade union focus. This is evidence that race equality is still seen as a separate, and secondary issue. Any discussion of anti-racism through labour politics in the 1990s needs to be aware of this.

The disciplinarity of labourism in the 1980s, in which policing the boundaries of labourism overtook policy generation, and in which local parties were suspended and individuals expelled, focused on Militant and not those demanding action on race politics (Astbury 1986: 17). With some exceptions, notably Sharon Atkin, black party activists managed to develop their political demands with minimal interference from labour's disciplinary machine. Quite why this occurred is not clear. Either labour was nervous of further antagonising those whose political demands were repeatedly marginalised, or black demands were regarded as a less serious threat to socialism than Militant's.

The 1980s produced, for the first time, a recognition of the significance of a black constituency in sustaining labourism in postwar politics. References to the 'black and Asian vote in a large number of key seats' (Labour Party 1985b: 3) acknowledges the debts of the past and looks to labour electability in the future. Labour's historic debt to black voters was reiterated from the constituencies – 'the black community expects more from the Labour Party which has enjoyed the favour of our loyal vote for over 40 years' (Johnson 1988: 107). The recognition of the importance of black support was sustained by a number of factors. Firstly, there were statements acknowledging that black demands required special attention, because racism was a specific problem. Listing the problems which black and white people suffered equally, the Labour Party (1980c: 1) officially acknowledged – 'But black people also face additional difficulties related to their colour'. This picks up some of the changes of the 1970s giving them official weight, suggesting that racism is a specific political problem requiring specific solutions, and, most important, committing labour to providing these solutions. Secondly, addressing racism required black involvement and not just black support. 'Labour and the Black Electorate' (Labour Party 1980c: 2–5) set out a strategy for developing black participation. Thirdly, recognition of a black constituency was sustained by an acknowledgement that labour had in the past failed adequately to represent black people. Through these outlined factors labour was constructing a picture of a black constituency demanding redress, and with a legitimate right to do so. It was to respond to what it understood this to mean, in developing its approach to race politics for the 1980s and 1990s.

RACE POLITICS TODAY

The basic contours of labour's race politics today were evident in the 1980s. Race issues in the 1980s did not have a central place in socialism, but they were not ignored. *Labour's Programme* (Labour Party 1982), a detailed policy statement prior to the review, gives reasonable coverage to race issues. Kinnock's (1987) statement in the election campaign of 1987 stated a commitment to dealing with racial disadvantage in employment. Some race dimensions of education received detailed treatment in labour's programme for multi-cultural education (Labour Party July 1989). Labour race politics still contained some familiar themes from the past. Labour's official preoccupation with immigration and nationality remained (Kinnock 1987, Labour Party 1981b, 1983a, 1982: 91–2). This was now highly critical of labour's 1960s dealings with immigration, a trend which began in the late 1970s (Messina 1989: 140). Public order remained a concern as the 1936 Public Order Act was replaced by the 1986 Public Order Act, into which labour had guided a broader definition of incitement to racial hatred. Race relations legislation was still deemed inadequate as a way of dealing with racism. The linking of fascism with racism was still evident into the mid-1980s, though not the prominent theme it had been in the 1970s.

Such analyses still insisted that labourism was a defence against fascism, which was fed by social deprivation (Tempia 1981: 252). Fascism was still occasionally linked with racial attacks, which remained a significant concern in race politics, though not attracting official support (Kelly 1985: 276, Merrell 1985: 277). Urban deprivation remained a race issue, underscored at various points by the uprisings in Toxteth, in Brixton and Moss Side which punctuated the 1980s (Labour Party 1983b). In general labour's race politics was still dominated by the concerns which emerged in the late 1970s (themselves conditions generated in the 1930s); social deprivation and inequitable social distributions were at the heart of labour's understanding of race issues. The key difference between the 1970s and the 1980s was that these old themes were subject to more detailed treatment.

There were also some significant shifts in labour's race politics in the 1980s. Firstly, labour signalled its intention to raise the political profile of race issues. When labour announced its 'new political offensive against racialism and racial disadvantage', it was in fact an old offensive, comprising as it did a commitment to deal with urban deprivation and race hatred, but announced with renewed political intent (Labour Party 1983b). Part of this intent was a more positive approach to multi-racialism 'not apologising for the black British but proclaiming the virtues and proclaiming the advantages and proclaiming the glories of a genuinely multi-racial society' (Hattersley 1982: 226). This was a greater enthusiasm for multi-racialism than had been shown by any previous labour Home Secretary, and signals intent to atone for the past whilst conceding no real policy changes. Messina claims that Hattersley was in fact a more progressive Home Secretary, and more interested in race issues than others, providing a 'subtle but tangible break with the past' (Messina 1989: 142). Certainly Hattersley was a product, if not the instigator, of the changes which had been taking place in labour's race politics from the late 1970s. His limitations, however, were evident in his blocking of democratic reforms calling for a bill of rights in 1987 as Rustin (1989: 40) notes. This could have been used as the basis from which to secure a commitment to black rights. Hattersley's limitations in race politics were also evident in his mishandling of the demand for black sections.

Secondly, renewed intent to deal with race was also evident in

146

labour's readiness to criticise its own track record on race politics. This is a distinctive feature of the 1980s and a marked break with past defensiveness. Immigration policy bore the brunt of labour's self-criticism (Lestor 1982: 227). In the early 1980s official statements began to repeat criticisms which had long been voiced by members in the constituencies. Labour's promise to repeal both the 1971 Immigration Act and the 1981 Nationality Act were discussed in chapter six.

Thirdly, the spectre of black revolt in the 1980s uprisings gave a new intensity to some old concerns about the 'pervasive discrimination against the black community' (National Executive Committee 1985). This had been publicised in the publication of the Scarman (1981) report. The re-eruption of Brixton in 1985 in the wake of the police shooting of Cherry Groce highlighted the fact that urban deprivation in that area had hardly been addressed and added to concerns about the state of tension between black communities and the police (National Executive Committee 1985). This conveyed the impression that the black community in Britain might be prepared to press its demands for social justice violently if their concerns were not attended to (Tempia 1981: 253).

The fourth important shift in labour's race politics in the 1980s, and part of the constraints producing other shifts (discussed briefly in the section dealing with conditions of emergence) was the significance attached to the black vote (Howe and Upshall 15 July 1988). Prominent warnings, reminding labour that fifty inner city parliamentary seats, and 200 local council seats had been made possible by black voters, were a distinctive feature of the 1980s (Patil 1988: 106). Such warnings were evidently needed officially, when the Labour Party (1986a: 1) acknowledged that in the 1983 general election there were thirty-seven 'ethnic marginals' [parliamentary seats] compared with only twenty-one in 1979 (see also Labour Party September 1989). Fear of the collapse of the black vote was certainly not solely responsible for labour's new attention to race issues, but it was a significant factor.

The fifth and most significant shift in labour race politics in the 1980s was the unprecedented level of black participation in local politics. This also had the effect of a constraint producing other changes, and was part of labour's recognition of a black constituency (discussed under the heading of conditions of emergence). The 1980s saw the emergence of black councillors, race relations advisors, a Race Committee at the Greater London Council, and a myriad of policies in education, social services and so on, aimed at improving access and quality of service delivery to local black populations. Spearheading the demands for equal opportunity in services was an impressive development of local black participation. 'The number of black councillors has trebled in the last four years and there are now over 200 black councillors in London alone' (Boyce 1986: 59). By 1987 Brent council in London had over twenty black councillors, and there were similar gains in other London councils, such as Hackney and Lambeth.

- Local black participation emerged around the development of local structures to deal with race equality. Ben-Tovim *et al.* (1986: 74–5) discuss some of these developments in the context of Wolverhampton and Liverpool. Liverpool, for example, had a race relations unit, a race relations sub-committee, a principal race relations advisor, and a multi-racial education unit. Similarly Wolverhampton with its equal opportunities policy, had a race relations committee containing representative from local Asian and Afro-Caribbean communities, a multi-cultural education service, and provided funding for various black community projects. The developments recorded by Ben-Tovim *et al.* are not atypical of the proliferation of race equality structures elsewhere. Ben-Tovim *et al.* warn that what appear to be local attempts to deal with race equality, often in fact render it ineffective and marginal. Similar warnings come from Ouseley (1990: 138–44) through his experiences in dealing with the Greater London Council.

Black involvement at the local level was not new in the 1980s. Black people had been involved in self-help projects in Britain since the 1960s and 1970s (Ben-Tovim *et al.*1986: 69–70, Abrams 25 June 1990). What was new in the 1980s was the extent of black involvement in town hall labour politics, and the proliferation of local structures to deal with racial equality. What was also new were the effects this had on local labourism. Local attempts at race equality may have provided only limited improvements in services delivered to black populations, as Solomos and Singh (1990: 95–114) warn in the context of housing. What is more significant is that these struggles with the local state through labour-run town halls, have produced a generation of experienced black local politicians and activists. Schooled by some harsh lessons in the politics of marginalisation, and suffering frustration at the blocks placed in the path of progress towards race equality, these local black activists have an unparalleled grasp of labourist political process, strategy and race-policy detail. Labour has unwittingly schooled a generation of experienced black politicians. This, and not marginal improvements in the lives of local black people, has been the effect of the 1980s attention to local race equality. These were the processes which produced Keith Vaz, Herman Ouseley, Diane Abbott, Bernie Grant, Kingsley Abrams and others. These highly experienced labourites are the most significant force shifting labour race politics in the 1980s. They are labour's most experienced race politicians.

Moves to make labour a multi-racial party undoubtedly were an extension of local black involvement in race politics. Labour took up this cause centrally and officially in 1980. The launch of the multi-racial party was signalled in 'Labour and the Black Electorate' (Labour Party 1980c) which set out a strategy to increase black involvement. Questionnaires were dispatched to local branches the same year, to collect information about the extent of black community involvement in local labour politics. (Labour Party 1980d). Such action was, of course, long overdue. Speeches from numerous conference platforms noted a lack of black delegates, especially from the trade unions (Boyce 1986: 60). There was widespread acknowledgement that political and social exclusion meant that black people were not well represented in the party, at the 'heart of British political life' (Goodman 1988: 106). 'The black community needs representation' (Johnson 1988: 107). There were few black representative images in the Labour Party. Black parliamentary candidates were not given safe labour seats to contest until 1987, when labour's first four black MPs went to Westminster.[1]

THE MULTI-RACIAL PARTY

The multi-racial party, and the form which black representation should take, was a central issue in labour's race politics in the 1980s, displacing other issues. An examination of what labour intended, officially, in its notion of the multi-racial party, the manner in which this was contested, and the implications of this for the development of an anti-racist politics, provide some significant issues to be addressed in the remainder of this chapter. Increasing black involvement in labour politics was not an unproblematic business. Large-scale black recruitment was always greeted in local branches with a suspicion that someone was empire-building (Sharma 1990). There were skirmishes in local branches over black section development, such as those in Birmingham Sparkbrook Constituency Labour Party, which led to some expulsions (Matharu 1986: 16).[2] What was labour's conception of the multi-racial party? And what was the political problem multi-racialism was designed to address?

There was a recognition throughout the party that black representation was a renewed attempt to deal with racial disadvantage. Black political organisation was to be at the centre of an anti-racist strategy – 'we all accept that black people have the right to organise in society, that their voice can and will be heard ...' (Goodman 1988: 106). Black participation would prioritise black issues, and offer black experience as a basis for political intervention (Labour Party 1985b, 1980c). Official support for black representation, and the building of a multi-racial party, was offered around the contention that black representation was more likely to produce effective anti-racist policies for the party, a task at which labour was officially admitting failure. Racial disadvantage, the result of labour's impotence, was thought to consist of low black living standards, a failure to replace racist immigration laws, a failure to deal with police harassment in black communities, a failure to provide adequate protection through race relations legislation and a failure to provide more than token representation for black people in the Labour Party. The way to address this catalogue of labour failure was the transformation of labour into a 'truly multi-racial party' (Labour Party 1980c). This required a more welcoming posture from the party, and the offer of a political voice, to what were perceived as voiceless black populations (Labour Party 1980c: 3)

Multi-racialism in the Labour Party was officially, and at the level of public declaration, about black empowerment and the development of effective anti-racist strategies. But it was also an insistence that labour was the most effective means of achieving black empowerment. Labour's offer of self-transformation as a means of addressing racism is a welcome departure in race politics, unthinkable in the 1960s, when labour even had problems with the idea of a multi-racial society, never mind a multi-racial party. Unfortunately, labour's conception of the multi-racial party did not effect black empowerment, it stifled it. It did not transform labour into an effective agency for anti-racist struggle, it marginalised anti-racism. It did not provide a means through which experienced black politicians, reared by labour around the town halls, could pursue the demands of Britain's black community for racial equality. Instead it excluded these people, and the political experience in dealing with race policies they brought with them. These points become clearer as we examine the debates around the demand for Labour Party black sections.

BLACK SECTIONS

The demand for black sections, as it emerged at labour conference, arose in the context of a debate about positive discrimination. The 1982 labour conference was presented with a vague resolution, calling for positive discrimination (whatever this might mean was not spelled out) in housing, employment and education, accompanied by a demand that labour give greater consideration to the views of 'ethnic minorities' in constructing policy (Sparkbrook Constituency Labour Party 1982: 224–5). This was supported by the National Executive and adopted by conference as party policy. Labour was now committed to positive action on race, with no traceable discussion as to what this might mean in practice. When positive discrimination emerged again at the 1983 conference, in an equally vaguely worded resolution, it was attached to a demand for black sections in the Labour Party (Hendon South Constituency Labour Party 1983: 260). National Executive support was not forthcoming on this occasion, and the resolution was remitted for further consideration. This conference marked a watershed in labour race politics, by producing an attempt to redefine the nature of the Labour Party, and by placing this important black demand on labour's political agenda.

Where this demand for black sections, and attempt to recast labourism came from is not entirely clear. Among significant influences are likely to be the Greater London Council, which, with its advisory committees on women and race issues, was cited as an example of good practice (Hendon South Constituency Labour Party 1983: 260). Other likely influences were the Labour Race Action Group (Messina 1989: 141).[3] Certainly Keith Vaz, the Labour Race Action Group's one-time chair, spoke in support of the 1983 conference resolution, suggesting that this group was involved in the demand for black sections. Other influences came from the Black Trade Union Solidarity Group (Sharma 20 July 1988). A most important source of demand for black sections is likely to be local black activists. This is supported by the fact that black sections are unofficially sustained in the constituencies, offering implicit acceptance of them, in areas where there is a significant black political presence. The demand for black sections was certainly brought to conference by the constituencies, and supported in the constituencies. Organisers of black sections also claim a certain political momentum from the 1980s uprisings (Abrams 25 June 1990).[4]

The demand for Labour Party black sections is blocked every year at conference by the National Executive and the trade union block vote. This ensures that it is repeatedly unsuccessful in its attempts to become party policy. This demand is met by various attempts on behalf of the National Executive to deal with it. The executive set up a working group to investigate the demand for black sections (Labour Party 1985b). The National Executive set up the Black and Asian Committee as an alternative and it has offered a black affiliated socialist society as another alternative. Labour has officially gone to great lengths not to accept the demand for black sections. The executive's latest strategy to stifle this demand is by an attempt to reform conference arrangements, so that the same issue cannot be debated every year (Abrams 25 June 1990).

The demand for black sections is not only persistent and persistently blocked, it is well supported. It is well supported by prominent black politicians. Black sections are seen as a source of momentum, generating and sustaining black participation (Balogun 1987: 134). Black MPs attribute their selection and support to the local work of black sections (Abbott 1988: 108).

Many local parties have black sections despite labour's refusal to make them official. The Black Sections Annual Conference reported that thirty constituencies had unofficial black sections by 1986 (Boyce 1986: 59). Labour's 1984 conference received twenty-three resolutions supporting black sections (Marwa 1984: 169). Every year the demand for black sections is passionately supported at conference in speeches by black members (Hyacinth 1987: 135). By 1986 unions were admitting to black sections, and their positive effect in building a black union membership (Sapper 1986: 60). Most important, the National Executive Committee's own working group, set up to investigate the demand for black sections, recommended that they be made official, following a survey in constituencies throughout the country which favoured black sections by a four to one majority (Labour Party 1985b: 12). Despite this overwhelming support for black sections throughout the labour movement, labour still officially refuses to recognise them and give them an official place in developing labour's race policy. This means that labour is attempting to construct a multi-racial party which excludes the form of representation most black members want. Labour's multi-racial party is to be a political agency which ignores the requirements of black members. This is an untenable position. What is it that black sections are demanding that labour finds so difficult to concede?

The demand for black sections is a demand to set up an organisational structure in the party for its black supporters.[5] The organisational structure of the black sections reflects that of the Labour Party itself. Local black sections have, where possible, representatives in local parties and on their executive and general committees. This provides a form of networking among black members, linked into the constituencies. Black section networks include black councillors, black council leaders, and from 1987 black MPs. Black sections, also like the Labour Party itself, have a regional structure, a national organising committee, a national conference, and a broad statement of political intent for discussion in the 'Black Agenda' (Labour Party Black Section 1988). Its national committee has a delegate structure from local parties, and various sub-committees: a women's committee, a trade union committee and a campaign committee (Abrams 25 June 1990). This mirrors labour's own organisational structure, with the exception that it is only open to those who define themselves as black. It is to this that the Labour Party most objects.

Black sections also stand for black mobilisation and black representative images in the party. Black organisation, networking and participation are perfectly consistent with official policy set out in 'Labour and the Black Electorate' (Labour Party 1980c). The demand for black sections is also an attempt to define a set of political priorities and approaches for labour.[6] Generally, the demand for black sections is an attempt to redefine labour's political priorities in the direction of broader social movements, which do not focus on labour's traditional workplace organisation. Workplace struggles have only a limited significance for black people, as they support only limited demands for racial equality (Abrams 25 June 1990). This general policy focus is not inconsistent with labourism which, in the policy review, takes on a breadth of concerns by means of a constituency organised by a conception of consumerism.

Socialism is one of the key commitments of the black sections. 'We have no choice but to be socialists', and in this 'black sections suffer from labourism' in supporting a similar political diversity (Abrams 25 June 1990). Black sections represent the entire spectrum of commitments to socialism, and share the belief that there is nothing to be gained from setting up a separate socialist party. Black sections' conceptions of socialism are set out in the 'Black Agenda'(Labour Party Black Section 1988) which was submitted to, and failed to influence, the policy review process. The Black Agenda offers an account of socialism which prioritises the analysis and elimination of racism. It reviews the forms of exclusion and disadvantage involved in immigration laws, policing, the inner city, social policy, employment, health, social services and education. It also provides an account of fascism and racial violence, the position of women, and offers a black perspective on international issues such as the struggles in Palestine and South Africa. It reviews existing structures of racism and makes recommendations for policy changes on a breadth of race issues to which official labourism has been unable to aspire. The Black Agenda's constituency is identified as 'blacks' (and not blacks and Asians) in which women are separated out as doubly oppressed, and in which youth are more militant in their potential for struggle. Blackness is construed in terms of a

154

multiplicity of oppressions, throughout British society and in a world sense, united by struggles against oppression all over the world. Its strategies are peaceful, involving policy changes to address racial disadvantage. Whilst these are not the terms of official labourism, concepts like oppression and struggle are certainly common currency on the left wing of labourism. The politics of the black sections fit comfortably within the limits of labourism, although it offers a challenge to official labourism in the extent to which it focuses on race concerns.

The Black Agenda is the black sections' official discussion document, and an umbrella for a diversity of black political voices. Other black voices, outside the Black Agenda stress other constituencies and priorities, and have their own forms of participation in mainstream labour politics. Russel Profitt stresses the potential of blackness in terms of political upheaval, attributed to youth in the uprisings in Brixton, Toxteth and elsewhere:

> The youth of Handsworth, Toxteth, Brixton and Southall know that they live in a multi-racial society, whether or not our leadership knows it. The question they ask, however, is when will they benefit from that? . . . Tell the black youth in Lewisham, East where I come from and where there are 100 people chasing every vacancy, that a Labour Party head office quango is the answer. They want a real say. That is what we are campaigning for in Lewisham, East. That was why I was endorsed. That is why we must support black sections.
>
> (Profitt 1985: 30–31)

Ben Bousquet[7] appeals to youth and upward mobility, in pointing out that black people did not come to Britain to join the ranks of the dispossessed, and challenges the classic left analysis that they are the lumpen proletariat:

> . . . the post War black migrant pioneers came to Britain not to join the ranks of the dispossessed indigenous classes, but to achieve that upward mobility which to an extent has been secured by their sisters and brothers in North America. In other words, and contrary to the muddled thinking of the white Left in this country, black people have never considered themselves to be the classic lumpen

proletariat much beloved by the Marxists – a class permanently consigned to endless pressure and the performance of inferior and socially demeaning roles.

(Bousquet 1987: 3)

Conceptions of socialism among the four black MPs (all supporters of black sections) who have to deal with labourism on a day to day basis across a range of issues, are also varied. Whilst the black sections executive, along with Abbott and Grant, backed the Benn/Heffer partnership in the labour leadership contest of the late 1980s, Boateng and Vaz supported Kinnock, claiming that the 'hard left' cannot deliver what black people want (Howe and Upshall 15 July 1988: 13). Socialism, like anti-racism, means many different things in the black sections. Which particular account and its constituencies will predominate remains to be seen. Clearly the black sections suffer from labourism, but this cannot be what labour is defending itself from, in fending off the demand for black sections as it does. Labour objects to a parallel form of labourism, which is exclusively for black members, and which is under black control.

THE BLACK AND ASIAN COMMITTEE

Labour's vision of the multi-racial party involved setting up the Black and Asian Committee, in place of the popularly supported black sections. The Black and Asian Committee was to give political expression to labour's multi-racialism, providing a vehicle for black representation in the party. It was the means by which labour's statements on the importance of black political participation (Labour Party 1980c, 1980d) were to be put into practice. The Black and Asian Committee was to divert the demand for black sections, and provide a form of black representation acceptable to the National Executive. In practice it increased the demand for black sections, and provided only a minimal form of black representation in the party. It was acceptable to the National Executive though, and remains an indictment of its conception of the multi-racial party.

The political rationale for black sections is set out in the minority report of labour's working group set up to consult the constituencies and make a recommendation about black representation (Labour Party 1985b).[8] The working group

156

recommended black sections, carrying a minority report prepared by those who disagreed. As the majority recommendation was unacceptable to the National Executive, the report was prefaced for publication by a National Executive statement supporting the minority report. It must be assumed from the attention paid to it, that the minority report's objections to black sections were highly significant for official labourism. These objections draw upon, and add to, the key arguments around at this point in the mid-1980s, and for this reason they are worth considering. Their significance is that they are an official labour statement on a key race issue in labour race politics at this time.

The minority report of the working party posed objections to black sections which concern matters of constituency and political priority.[9] The minority report represents that strand of labourism which has its roots in the 1930s, and which has, historically, provided an opposition to the assertion of race as a political priority. It recalls the political tension points of the 1970s, when labour officially conceded that racism was a political problem requiring a specific form of politics, in accepting that racial hatred was a significant issue. This position was reasserted by the National Executive in 'Labour and the Black Electorate' (Labour Party 1980c: 1) in its recognition that the forms of disadvantage suffered by black people made them a specific constituency of the working class. The executive's support for the minority report of the working group is a retreat from this position, already established within the boundaries of official labourism. The minority report insists that the demand for racial equality be incorporated into the more general framework of a class politics. 'Some of us', it declared, 'believe that the interests of blacks are inseparable from those of the working class' (Labour Party 1985b: 36). This establishes a ranking of political priorities, in which race struggles are presented as endangering and dividing socialist commitment (Sourani 1986: 61, Apps 1985: 33). At the level of constituencies, this incorporates black socialists into the working class as a whole, and leaves them without a form of politics to address the specific dimensions of racial disadvantage.

This assertion, that class politics were the only legitimate basis for developing a socialist strategy, was also extended to the political agency representing a class politics, the Labour Party itself. The minority report declares that 'on principle a socialist party should not be divided on racial grounds' (Labour Party 1985b: 36). Official labourism's most serious objection to black sections is that they are black, and provide a form of organisation which excludes white labour members. Despite long acknowledgement, even by central enunciative sites in the party, that skin colour was a basis for social division and social inequality, skin colour could not be accepted as a basis for political organisation to address those social divisions. This is the more ironic in the light of the analysis offered in this study. This suggests that labour itself construed the social and political significance of blackness, in terms of a range of negative significances. Labour's own construction of blackness in the 1950s, 1960s and early 1970s, which required the defence of the political community from the bearers of black skin, gave significant political direction and support to a structure of black inequalities in postwar Britain. It is ironic that labour now refuses to concede skin colour as the basis of political organisation, when labour itself was responsible for constructing the social and political significance of blackness. Labour's crime is not that it supported racist immigration controls (though of course it did), or that it provided only ineffective protection for black citizens in its attempts at race relations legislation. These are insignificant by comparison to its conceptualisation of Britain as a political community in which the co-existence of blacks and whites was a force for disruption, violence and competition. Labour has never acknowledged its part in constructing the significance of blackness in these terms, and it now refuses to accept, as a basis for political organisation, the social and political divisions it created and sustained through labour race politics.

Labour's multi-racial party could not admit separate black representation. The Black and Asian Committee, which emerged from the National Executive statement which appeared with the working group report, was to provide a form of black representation which included white party members.[10] In fact the Black and Asian Committee was not a discovery of the working group at all. It was mooted as a possibility in 1983, when the demand for black sections first emerged at conference. This indicates that the executive had already decided on the form black representation in the party should take. Quite why it went to the trouble of setting up a working group, only to ignore its recommendations, is not clear. The Black and Asian Committee was announced by Hattersley (1985: 37–38) as the form of black representation appropriate for a multi-racial Labour Party. Even its name presented a controversial division of blackness 'dividing the common struggle' (Patil 1988: 106). Its name was taken to imply that racism, which requires the term black to indicate a collectivity of victims, was not the main issue to be addressed. The Black and Asian Committee's remit was to increase black membership and participation within the party, promote discussion on race and make race a more central party issue. Its secretary Virendra Sharma became labour's ethnic minorities officer in 1986.

The Black and Asian Committee was intended to be ineffective. Its initially rather weak advisory status was only later upgraded when it was made a full committee of the National Executive in 1987. Lack of resourcing presented constant difficulties. It was not consulted by the Parliamentary Labour Party, or the National Executive, over race issues. Trade union members and personnel from central enunciative sites in the party rarely turned up for meetings. Far from making race a priority, the committee issued not a single major statement on race, and was by-passed totally by labour race policy-making. The committee had a structure of black representation from the constituencies, organised on a regional basis. This, however, did not work well as a networking system, because it focused on party headquarters, and not on local organisation and black grass roots community action. It relied on representatives being able to get time off work, and get to London for meetings. In practice this arrangement gave the committee very poor black networks. There were hints at conference that the committee remained obscure as far as local black organisation was concerned (Balogun 1987: 134). By 1990 the committee's secretary and party's ethnic minorities officer had resigned claiming that the Labour Party just wanted an 'office boy' to deal with race (Sharma 20 June 1990). This episode of the Black and Asian Committee is an indictment of labour's official conception of the multi-racial party.

The most serious problem with the Black and Asian Committee, and ultimately the reason it failed so dismally, was that it failed seriously to address the demand for black representation.

The committee antagonised those whose political aspirations it should have addressed, the voices demanding black section representation. It was variously described as 'patronising and tokenistic' (Johnson 1988: 107), 'the unselected, the unaccountable and the tame' (Balogun 1987: 134), as 'undemocratic, consisting of appointees, the great, the good and the unaccountable' and 'set up to undermine black sections' (Belos 1986: 60). The committee was boycotted by those who supported black sections. Among these were black council leaders, and other experienced local black politicians, who could have provided the expertise labour needed in developing an effective anti-racist political stance for the 1990s. The Black and Asian Committee was wound up after the 1989 conference. Labour still lacks an official form of black representation.

The fate of the Black and Asian Committee is a powerful reminder of the gap between declarations of intent, and practical structures for action in the political process. Labour's stated conception of the multi-racial party promised a welcoming posture, an increase in black membership, links with black constituency organisations, black representative images at the commanding heights of the party, and policies to address racial inequality. In practice, and practice is a powerful form of statement, a quite different multi-racial party was provided. Labour's multi-racial party was not prepared to listen to the demands of its black members for separate representation in the party. Labour's multi-racial party could not concede that racial distinction, though a basis for social division, was a legitimate basis for political organisation. Labour's multi-racial party was not genuinely interested in building black membership, or it would not have stifled the only political agency (black sections) to have made any gains in this direction. Labour's multi-racial party was one in which race issues were dealt with by a committee which did not make policy, and which did not involve influential black political leaders, or those from major enunciative sites in the party. Officially, labour really wanted to maintain the marginality of race as a political issue, whilst at the same time confronting it in the way least threatening to labourism. The gap between statement and action is an important one, but statement is a vital starting point in the political process.

CONCLUSION

Labour's handling of the race concept and its grasp of anti-racism have seen some important changes in the 1980s. This volume has demonstrated that race, racism and anti-racism are political constructs, generated and sustained in discourses concerned with populations designated with reference to racial difference. Race, as a form of distinction, is commonly organised around the specification of political communities and the principles upon which they are construed. Racial difference and its anatomical indicators have no significance, but are assigned a meaning and a force in political discourse. This process occurs around the discursive association between race and a field of concepts which give it a significance. Significance is established and construed around political projects and principles. Labour contributed a field of concepts and significances to racial difference in British politics which now needs to be reformed. This process has begun with the reformulation of political principles which recast, in a more positive light, the political value of multi-racialism. It is the social and political meaning and value attached to human difference which is at the root of inequality.

The multi-racial party was a central element in labour's anti-racism. Its claim to be a political agency for reform, providing racial equality, must therefore be reviewed in the context of its conception of a multi-racial party. Official labourism's retreat into class politics, in denying the importance of racism, whilst at the same time asserting its specificity and significance as a political issue, indicates that labourism is a mass of contradictory positions when it comes to race. Positions can be won at the level of declaration, and then lost at the level of implementation, as in the 1970s shift in providing official recognition that race hatred was an important issue. Positions can be implemented in practice, without seeming to present an enunciative challenge to party policy, as in the case of local action around racial attacks in the 1930s and in the 1970s. There are no central and enduring principles or rationales sustaining and directing labourism as a political process. Even recurring themes like support for democracy can be as diverse and contradictory as the claims made upon it. Political interventions are constructed around principles, and can be revealed through an analysis of political discourse, but these principles can be reconstructed and reformed. This was apparent in labour's construction of the political community around its anxieties about multi-racialism's capacity for the proper practice of political association. This guided labour's early immigration and race relations policies, but was reformulated in the 1970s, and further developed in the 1980s as black people become a labour constituency.

Labour's future as a force for racial equality in British politics is an open question. This study has shown that labour race politics were constructed and reconstructed from the 1930s. It has mapped labour's treatment of race issues in postwar Britain in terms of their conditions of emergence in the 1930s, and their transformations along the way. The political processes in which transformations occur are impossible to predict. They are dynamic, and rely on active forces and political agencies to effect them. Labour has taken some important steps in the direction of reformulating race politics in the 1970s and 1980s. It has retreated under pressure from the demand for black representation which requires a more powerful input on race issues into labourism than labour is prepared to concede. But this is no reason to conclude that labour is forever incapable of giving political direction to anti-racism. Labour has moved from giving political direction to racism, to a position which acknowledges the need for effective anti-racist strategies, even if it has so far blocked their development. Labourism is, in terms of philosophy, policy, strategy and commitment to constituencies, capable of giving political expression to anti-racist politics. It has a notion of social justice, and a conception of citizenship which can support a demand for black rights. But the political forces which can insist on implementing what has been accepted within the boundaries of official labourism have been thwarted in their political demands. Black sections' activists are the political force pressing these demands in the 1990s, along with the small group of labour MPs in parliament. What they will provide, and how they will reform labourism remains to be seen. Whatever the political gains they can wrest from labourism, four million black

Britons, whose lives are enmeshed in racist allocation procedures, will be watching labour's performance when next it forms a government. If labour's conceptions of democracy, order, justice and citizenship are to be meaningful, they must as a matter of urgency address politically the social position of black Britons.

NOTES

INTRODUCTION

1 This study is concerned with the ways in which social and political categories are generated and sustained. Its general approach is hence influenced by the work of Cutler, Hindess, Hirst and Hussain (1977). Its approach to race politics was developed in the context of the City University Race, Culture and Policy Research Unit.

2 This point is made by Foucault (1972), though not in relation to race. The general point is that concepts are constructed in discourse.

3 Political community is a concept which has its intellectual roots in pluralist sociology (Kuper and Smith 1971) and the work of political philosophers like Rousseau (1973) and Locke (1970). It is not always a term of the discourse, but a principle underlying the discourse, organising a series of concepts which have a bearing on race. It will be explored more fully as the arguments in this volume are developed.

1 EXPLORING RACE AND LABOURISM: A CONCEPTUAL FRAMEWORK

1 Comparative philology is the comparative study and classification of languages. It led to the rethinking of forms of racial classification and boundaries constructed through eighteenth-century anthropology. It gained currency as a form of classification in the period 1850 to 1870 and produced the category 'Indo-European' as an alliance of Indian and European races. It supported the case that certain Indians were equal to Europeans in culture and civilisation (Leopold 1974: 578–603).

2 Eighteenth-century anthropology involved the classifications of Cuvier and the other French anatomists. They divided human beings on the basis of a range of phenotypical features, but prioritised cranial measurement, which was taken as indicative of brain capacity (Stocking 1969: 39–41). These notions of racial difference were not superseded by those offered by comparative philology, but the two systems of racial classification co-existed as late as 1930, when they were evidently used in labour discourse to discuss Indian independence.

3 Foucault's general theory of knowledge divides the world into the discursive and the non-discursive. It suggests that anything which can be known is spoken about. In being spoken, things enter the domain of discourse. All knowledge, therefore, is gained through the study of discourse, as the place where concepts and objects (and what they reveal about the world) are registered.

4 The notion of a constraint, though it exists in Foucault's work, is best developed by Cutler *et al.* (1977) where it is employed for different purposes from those in this volume. In this study a constraint is anything which imposes a direction on discourse. Constraints may include political circumstances, other statements, political continuity, a particular understanding of the audience to which a statement is addressed, or a site from which a statement is made. The constraints producing a given set of concepts, constitute their conditions of emergence.

5 The text contains the discourse. It is the place where discourses are registered and made available for analysis. Texts may be identified in terms of whom they address, their audience, the site from which they are issued, and the political objectives and voices articulated. Texts do not carry equal weight in labour discourses. Official policy-bearing texts obviously have a greater weight than unofficial or minority statements.

6 The 'working class racism thesis' was a product of academic work on race in the 1970s. It was cogently explored in Miles and Phizacklea (1979a) in their essay on 'Working Class Racist Beliefs in the Inner City'. For many marxists the discovery of working class racism was a problem. It led to the theorisation of racism as a strategy of capital used to divide the working class. The political implications of this was to see the Labour Party as a barometer of racism in its constituency, the working class.

7 A much more detailed critique is supplied by Cambridge and Feuchtwang (1990: 27–58).

8 The term 'black marxist' refers to a perspective, developed from within a marxist framework, which prioritises black over class politics, and not to self-designation or the skin colour of its authors. However, most of the published supporters of this stance would identify themselves as black.

9 The term constituency derives from political philosophy. It refers to those who are represented, or who are claimed to be represented, by a political statement or position. Labourist discourse invokes a range of constituencies, for example, workers, trade unionists, the working class, black people, women and so on. These are simply claims. They may be contested by others who may claim to represent different politics and the 'true' interests of black people, workers and so on. Of course there is no such thing as a true set of interests, and any alliance between a population category and a set of political object-ives (for example civil rights on behalf of black Britons) is simply a claim constructed between constituencies and political demands in discourse.

10 Political objectives refer to the demands stated on behalf of a constituency. They are explained in the context of constituencies in note 9.

11 The exceptions to this are Ben-Tovim *et al.* (1986), Solomos (1989) and Ball and Solomos (1990). Whilst these accounts are not centrally concerned with labourism, all provide excellent and detailed accounts of race equality measures in local politics, and the political processes surrounding them.

12 Race relations policy and immigration are coupled and prioritised in labourist discourse on race, so it is not surprising that these are key issues taken up by academic writing on race and the Labour Party.

2 SOCIALISM IN THE 1930s AND FOR THE 1990s

1 Policy definitions of socialism are also philosophical claims, but they are distinguished by their main purpose, which is to set out in detailed terms a particular course of political action, usually through legislation or changes in practice, policy or procedure.

2 See Labour Party (1933a) 'Socialism and the Condition of the People.'

3 See the Society for Socialist Inquiry and Propaganda publication by Cole (1931) *For those Over 21 Only.* The society was formed in 1931, at the same time as the New Fabian Research Bureau. The task of

labour intellectuals in the bureau was to translate socialist thinking into legislative form, whilst the society publicised its pronouncements through pamphlets, education and advice to local councils (New Fabian Research Bureau 1931, Society for Socialist Inquiry and Propaganda 1932).

4 See Lansbury (1929–1935). These personal papers of Lansbury reveal the influence of Methodism and a social welfare perspective on socialism in this particular kind of labourism.

5 Guild Socialism, at its height in the 1920s when the building guilds were in operation, involved a conception of industrial democracy which involved direct producers in decision-making. The guilds had declined by the 1930s, but the ideals on which they were based were in evidence in labourist discourses in that period, and associated most closely with the work of G.D.H. Cole.

6 Although opinion within the Labour Party on the Soviet Union differed considerably, officially sanctioned opinion tended towards the views expressed by Durbin, that it was a repressive and inhuman regime. 'It is twenty years since the Communist Party gained undisputed power in Russia. Still the victims tramp down to death. There is no end to the suffering, the river of blood flows on' (Durbin 1940: 218). Labour's official relationship with the Communist Party was structured by this kind of pronouncement. Unofficially there was some co-operation.

7 This refers to co-operation with labour and socialist organisations in other countries. Labour's commitment to peace had to be abandoned later in the 1930s, in defence of democracy which was threatened by European fascism. Labour's commitment to peace has been stated and re-stated since the 1930s, but is always ambivalent and contingent.

8 Bertrand Russell and particularly Leonard Woolf were the chief architects of labour's foreign and colonial policy. Woolf was part of the British colonial administration in Ceylon, through which he had a detailed grasp of colonial policy in operation. Woolf's view of labour international policy is set out in an article in *Political Quarterly* (1933) and his book, *Imperialism and Civilisation*, published in the same year.

9 The records of the National Executive Committee for 1930 contain a resolution for conference, demanding support for Indian political prisoners, submitted by a constituency party. It was sent back for amendment many times before it was acceptable to the National

167

Executive and backed by them at conference. My comments on the conditions of authorisation of statements are drawn from the executive's requirements in respect of this resolution being made suitable for official sanction.

10 The National Joint Council existed before 1930 as a forum for discussion between the Parliamentary Labour Party and the trade union movement. In 1930 it was formally constituted as the National Joint Council, and in 1934 it was re-named the National Council of Labour. This committee was always trade union dominated. The Trades Union Congress held more seats than either the Parliamentary Labour Party, or the National Executive Committee, and the reports of their meetings show that discussions were dominated by trade union issues (National Joint Council 1934a).

11 The Labour Government, formed in 1929, resigned in 1931 following the report of the May Committee, which insisted on cutting government expenditure on unemployment. Ramsey MacDonald and the other Labour Nationalists then formed the National Government, as a coalition of parliamentary forces. They were promptly expelled from the Labour Party.

12 The Independent Labour Party was encouraged to distance itself from the Labour Party by other members of the League Against Imperialism, which was disgusted by labour's colonial policy, and especially their treatment of Indian political prisoners. The Independent Labour Party's programme is set out in Fenner Brockway's work (1928, 1931).

13 Fenner Brockway (author's interview 1977) admitted that the decision to split from the Labour Party had been wrong.

14 See, for example, Labour Party (1933b) and National Joint Council (1933b).

15 See Labour Party (1988, 1989).

16 Production and consumption are key concepts emerging from the policy review, supporting a bifurcated citizenship of producers and consumers. Labour's attention to consumption is not new, but never before has it had so high a profile or been linked to a statement of rights.

17 Charter 88 provided an important challenge to labourist notions of democracy in the late 1980s. The charter was published in November 1988, on the three-hundredth anniversary of the revolution of 1688 which laid the basis for the current parliamentary system. It is a non-party, citizen's movement, but some of its more prominent

activists operate in, or on the fringes of the Labour Party. Its key demands include a bill of rights to guarantee basic democratic freedoms such as the right to free association, peaceful assembly, freedom from discrimination, freedom from detention without trial, trial by jury, privacy and freedom of expression. The charter is also a demand for the modernisation and reform of the electoral system including freedom of information, open government, proportional representation, reform of the upper house and an independent, reformed judiciary (Charter 88 May 5–6 1990: 15).

18 Labour's European Community does not involve any blurring of national boundaries. In fact it provides the opportunity for the re-statement of a national identity for Britain, in a competitive sense of getting the best deal for British workers and pensioners (Labour Party 1989: 7).

19 There is evidence of strong feminist influence and interests evident throughout the report of the policy review (Labour Party 1989: 33, 29, 30).

20 This is an advance on the policy review statement of 1988 which explicitly presents racial equality as a European issue, best pursued through the European Court of Human Rights.

3 THE LABOUR PARTY'S COMMONWEALTH

1 Community, and consideration of racially plural societies, occurred in anthropology in relation to the withdrawal of colonial rule (see Furnival 1939). In Kuper's (1971) work the construction of political community is inseparable from the problematic of social order. Pluralism was a term used by a variety of social theorists to refer to societies where there were several principles of existence, co-existing within a single political framework. Political constructions of multi-racialism draw upon this kind of intellectual basis. The notion of community is developed within political philosophy by Maine (1965), Locke (1970), Montesquieu (1949) and Hobbes (1970), who all developed notions of community and speculate on the origins of community and the nature of social bonds.

2 Political community should not be confused with constituencies which are the groups within a single political community around which political demands are advanced.

3 India had been publicly promised independence by the Montagu Chelmsford Declaration of 1917, and the Government of India Act of

1919. This in turn established the authority of the Royal Commission of 1930 (see Home Affairs Department 1930) to report on conditions in India, with a view to framing an appropriate constitution. It would be difficult for any government to retreat from these pledges, though they were open to a variety of interpretations and time-scales.

4 Even colonial India had not been a single political entity. The Indian States ruled by the princes had never been entirely subjected to the authority of the King/Emperor. The states were formally independent territories, but their rulers had agreed to attend the Round Table Conference with a view to forming a part of independent India. In fact, a disproportionate amount of time was spent at the Round Table, hammering out the arrangements between any independent government in India, and the Indian states.

5 The Moslem League also supported this claim of racial distinctiveness in asserting a separate nationhood.

6 The oral history archives at the Nehru Library in Delhi, which record the views of congress leaders and Indian trade unionists, and the written documents, statements and letters between Provincial Congress leaders, all indicate an intense, if uneven, level of nationalist disruption throughout India. Two impressions emerge from these sources: the extent of hatred of the British presence in India, and the savagery with which Indian uprisings were repressed. British strategies included the unpopular lathi (baton) charges into crowds and transporting agitators miles out of town so that they had to walk back.

7 The activities under the formal direction of the congress were varied. The best-known protests were the salt-making campaign, the foreign cloth boycott, and the picketing of liquor shops. Protest activities were conducted on a district basis in camps run by volunteers, who were answerable to the District Dictator. Districts linked up within each state, and the states with the National Congress. The quote below, from the Bihar Provincial Congress Committee to the All India Congress Committee, indicates the extent of local support for civil disobedience in that area, and the extent of police activity. Other areas did not report such high levels of activity, indicating that it must have been uneven.

> Many districts have altogether been deprived of their prominent workers, but the work is being carried on as usual by those left behind for the movement has gone deep down to the masses and it is from them, from those uneducated village folk that

our workers are drawn and they form the real backbone of the movement. . . . Total arrests during the week six hundred and ten and total up to 18th July three thousand seven hundred and eighty two.

(All India Congress Committee 18 July 1930)

8 The centrality of labour in Indian independence is demonstrated in the extensive output of Woolf in the Imperial Advisory Committee (labour's main forum for colonial policy), the oral and written history archives at the Nehru Library, Delhi (See All India Congress Committee 1929–1939), and by Mesbahuddin's (1989) detailed account of the 1920s and 1930s.

9 This was an international watchdog over colonial affairs and critic of the Labour Party's approach to the colonies. Founded around 1927, it was supported by the Communist International and shunned by the Labour Party (Labour Party 1930a). Its British section, headed by Colonel Bridgeman at this time, contained Independent Labour Party members, Communist Party members and trade unionists. The League was instrumental in forcing the Independent Labour Party's split with the Labour Party in the early 1930s.

10 The term delegate is misleading. Indian delegates to the Round Table Conference were selected by the British (labour) Government. The Indian Statutory Commission and Royal Commission on Labour in India provided the basis for deciding who should be invited. The list of delegates was, in some ways, slightly different from the populations which were enfranchised with independence in 1947.

11 The Royal Commission on Labour in India was served by prominent British trade unionists and members of the Labour Party. Its focus was to identify an industrial working class from the peasantry, and the processes by which they could be developed to citizenship through reforms in their working conditions.

12 These are average rates. They are obtained by adding together the seats for each community or population in each province and dividing by the total number of provinces in order to give a national picture.

13 The size of the franchise was estimated by the Indian Trades Union Federation (the organisation created by the Labour Party to represent workers) and is indicated in various documents released during the 1930s up to the Government of India Act 1935 (see, for example, Trades Union Federation 1933–1935).

4 ANTI-SEMITISM IN EAST LONDON

1 The main intellectual forces operating in the British Union of Fascists were not just anti-semitic, though this may have been its most popular doctrine, but of a kind of corporatism Mosley developed out of his involvement in labour policy-making with Lansbury. Corporatism emphasises unity over class division. The British union also propounded a strident nationalism, and considered the nation the natural form for race supremacy. The British Union were strident defenders of empire (See Skidelsky 1975).

2 Methodism and labourism in East London were intimately connected through social activities, through the Methodist Sunday school which met at Lansbury's house in Bow, and through a commitment to the socially disadvantaged and the cause of social reform (Benningfield 1977. See also Lansbury's personal papers 1929–1935, held at the British Library of Political and Economic Science).

3 Jewishness was constructed in political discourse through labour's dealings with anti-semitism, though this should not be taken to mean that these were priorities for labour, which was preoccupied with fascism and haggling with the Communist Party. The term anti-semitism was commonly used in the 1930s, as were racial and racialism, but not racism.

4 Englishness was a term of the discourse and used in connection with notions of racial difference, though the idea of an English race had only a shadowy existence in these discourses. It featured as the 'other' against which Jewishness was constructed. East End Englishness had particular characteristics.

5 Statements in the *New Statesman and Nation* were not necessarily labour statements, but this publication took up issues which were discussed in the Labour Party. It also contains more analytic accounts than are found in conference or parliamentary statements, and is therefore a useful source of fragments of discourse.

6 The Poale Zion or Jewish Labour Party was a distinct organisation, though affiliated to the Labour Party in the 1930s. Of course the Labour Party and trade unions also had Jewish members, often in prominent positions.

7 Some labour and Independent Labour Party members took up the cases of individual Jewish refugees. Fenner Brockway (1977) admitted to having aided refugees to obtain forged passports and entry documents in order to escape Nazi persecution.

8 The Jewish Ex-Servicemen, who would parade in medals won fighting for King and country in the first world war and were often disabled, were organised into vigilante groups and operated a form of Jewish self-defence in East London.

9 It is not that labour was calling for the repatriation of Jews to Palestine, but it supported this which was also the cause of the Poale Zion, the Board of Deputies of Anglo Jewry and the wish of many British Jews (Levenberg 1977). This does, however, indicate a reluctance to entertain the prospect of a racially plural society, especially in the context of pitched battles between fascists and anti-fascists over the Jewish presence in many large cities.

10 Despite officially supporting the demand for a Jewish territory in Palestine, labour managed to antagonise broad sections of Jewish opinion all over the world, in its handling of the Palestine mandate after the second world war. The Poale Zion fell out with labour as Jewish refugees, who had suffered the worst holocaust in human history, were kept waiting in refugee camps whilst labour fumbled with the issue of Palestine (Levenberg 1977).

5 RACE AND RACE RELATIONS IN POSTWAR BRITAIN

1 Ennals (1976: 221) commented that there would be as few as ten labour MPs in the Commons for a major debate on race at that time.

2 Hendon South Constituency Labour Party kindly allowed me easy access to their records, and for this I thank them. They contain little mention of race issues despite the fact that this is an area of Jewish and Asian settlement and, until the mid-1970s, had been the scene of anti-fascist campaigns and the Grunwick dispute. There is no reason to suspect that it was atypical of other constituencies. It is likely that race was only discussible in a certain way in the Labour Party at this time.

3 As late as 1977 the terms coloured, black and immigrant were all used at Labour Party conferences to refer to black people.

4 The term ethnic was a term of the discourse on race which featured in the Race Relations Acts, as an attempt to be inclusive of all minority populations. It was not commonly used to signal difference within black populations until the 1980s. Ethnic received some use around the arrival of Ugandan Asians in the early 1970s, indicating that they were regarded as different from other immigrants. Ugandan Asians were identified by Conservatives in the

173

parliamentary debates of this time, as law-abiding and industrious in contrast to other immigrants. Labour mainly focused on their wealth.

5 Urban funding came via Section 11 of the Local Government Act (1966) to provide funding for teachers and social workers to address the problem of 'immigrant integration' and focused on language difficulties. The Local Government Grant (Social Needs) Act (1969), under the Urban Programme, provided nursery schools, teachers' centres, family advice centres and voluntary play groups. These two measures were later supplemented by the Inner Urban Areas Act (1978) which was preceded by the partnership agreements. All were an attempt to fund areas deemed stressed by the arrival of immigrants. They offer a particular contextualisation for blackness.

6 As Ben-Tovim and Gabriel (1984) point out, the weaknesses of the 1976 Race Relations Act include the problem involved in identifying the effects of indirect discrimination and a lack of enforcement powers, to ensure the complicity of local authorities in implementing equal opportunity legislation.

7 The rights and freedoms of the indigenous population formed the backdrop against which the multi-racial political community was constructed, through race relations legislation. There was parliamentary concern that the limited protection from racial discrimination offered by the legislation would encroach on the freedom of expression of the indigenous population. The 1965 bill, especially, was accompanied by a parliamentary debate which was concerned with the limitation placed by the bill on the rights of publicans to refuse and exclude patrons. This was not Britain's first piece of equal opportunity legislation. Racial discrimination in employment in the Indian civil service was incorporated into the Government of India Bill 1833, and reinforced by the Indian Civil Service Act (1861) and the Government of India Act (1919). Like the 1960s legislation, this had a minimal impact. Between 1919 and 1929 the number of Indians in the civil service trebled from 78 to 241 (Lester and Bindman 1972: 379).

8 References to Englishness through historical association, are found in the second reading of the 1965 Race Relations Bill by the Labour Home Secretary (Soskice 1965b: 933). Englishness was a way of designating membership of the political community of the nation, usually through reference to some historical association, thus staking a claim on indigenousness.

6 LABOUR AND IMMIGRATION FROM THE 1950s TO THE 1990s

1 Immigration laws are also linked to nationality laws. The 1981 Nationality Act substantially amended the 1971 Immigration Act. The increasing stringency of immigration laws was also commonly linked in labour discourse to the, rather limited, demands for racial equality, contained in the three Race Relations Acts (of 1965, 1968 and 1976). It was argued that restriction protected immigrants already settled in Britain, as did race relations legislation.

2 Of course black immigration to Britain affected British politics long before the postwar period as Solomos (1989: 35–9) points out. Understandings of the political significance of blackness were also developed around Indian independence, as this study has shown. But by the 1950s we see the dominance of the discursive clustering race, immigrant and coloured (later black) as significant concepts in labour discourse.

3 The term indigenous is obviously problematic as a description of people who do not claim recent immigrant roots. Indigenous is not a term of discourse, but a principle underlying the construction of political communities, and used to establish a hierarchy of claims upon a nation's resources. Non-immigrant might be a better term, but historically all Britons are immigrants. The term Englishness is sometimes used to establish claims to indigenousness, and this was discussed in chapter five and its note 8. It was the concept immigrant that produced particular notions of Englishness and indigenousness in the postwar period. The one was defined in relation to the other, in the context of constructing a political community, and within it a hierarchy of claims upon its resources.

4 From 1962 to 1981 British immigration legislation was out of step with citizenship laws. The 1981 Nationality Act brought citizenship into line with immigration, making Britain the only country in the world who had citizens with no right of abode.

5 The 1948 Nationality Act conferred Britishness on citizens of the UK, its colonies and commonwealth, meaning that black commonwealth immigrants were formally British, though obviously never regarded as British in the same sense as the indigenous population. The 1962 Commonwealth Immigrants Act formally bifurcated the Britishness constructed in 1948, though this was a unitary category in name only. The myriad debates in the 1950s indicate that Britishness was in fact constructed around commonwealth and its implicit inequalities, as this chapter argues.

175

6 Employment needs were discussed in the context of immigration. So too were the economic pressures which forced people to migrate, and the constraints of commonwealth obligation. We begin to see the discursive ascendancy of capacity-to-absorb arguments linking social reform and economic conditions in Britain.

7 East African Asians were widely considered to be professionals, and hence more absorbable into British society (Davis 1972: 868). East African Asians were different from other immigrants, because they were refugees (Lyon 1976a: 58). But East African Asians were also a focus for resentment by labour MPs from poor urban constituencies, because they were suspected of being wealthy, and yet draining public resources in Britain through the cost of resettlement camps. The cost of the East African Asian Resettlement Board and camps were an issue raised a great deal in parliament in the early to mid-1970s.

8 Patriality refers to a specific form of connectedness to Britain. It refers to those who are born, naturalised or adopted in the UK or who have a parent or grandparent who was born, naturalised or adopted there.

9 The 1971 Immigration Act, as Rose (1973: 183–96) points out, effectively severed the connection between immigration and work.

10 The concept immigrant was also significantly constructed in the 1970s around notions of legality and illegality. These concerns obviously throw the spotlight of suspicion on immigrants as a whole, as who was to know who was legal and who illegal? Even legally settled immigrants were implicated in these concerns, because they were suspected of sustaining illegal immigrants. Williams (1973: 1405–13) makes this connection between legal and illegal immigrants, a most damaging association providing a rationale for raids on black communities, like the passport raids. There were no official figures indicating the extent of illegal immigration, save for those deported and no doubt suspected of being the tip of an iceberg. Hence illegal immigration was open to speculation and ever-increasing public anxiety. Labour, at least officially, attempted to suggest that reports of illegals were exaggerated, but nevertheless issued statements saying it would deal with illegal immigration, which it linked to fears about taking British jobs, especially in the hotel and catering industry (Summerskill 1972: 1995–2000) which needed to be protected in periods of high unemployment.

11 The five categories of British citizenship are: British protected persons; British subjects without citizenship; British overseas citizenship; citizenship of British dependent territories; and British citizenship (the only category carrying the right of abode). This sustains the significance of the commonwealth.

7 ANTI-RACISM IN THE 1930s

1 Racism and anti-semitism are used interchangeably in this chapter. Race and racism are terms imposed on the discourse in order to make an analysis. Of course any strategy addressing racial disadvantage may be thought of as anti-racist and this is the sense in which it is used in this study.

2 We are less concerned about whether the Labour Party was anti-semitic, than with how it construed political categories like Jewishness, and how it addressed anti-semitism. It certainly seems that labour's approach to anti-semitism constituted both a failure to defend Jews as a racially persecuted group, and that in many ways Jewish people were seen as a problem by labour. This may be seen as a form of racism, in that it was likely to contribute to negative assessments of Jewish people in terms of their impact on Britain, and hence contribute to their exclusion and disadvantage in British society. Labour may be accused of constructing its own forms of racial disadvantage, and of a failure to defend, but this is quite different from making anti-semitic statements.

3 An example of anti-semitism in the form of verbal attacks on the Jewish population from a labour platform, is found through correspondence between Labour Party headquarters and Richard Davies, prospective parliamentary candidate for the Plymouth area. This correspondence refers to a speech Davies made in Tavistock, and reported in the *Western Morning News* under the heading 'British Labour Candidate attacks Jews' (National Executive Committee 1933). This was the cause of a reprimand from Transport House, and in the ensuing correspondence Davies (May 1933) reaffirmed his position on the Jewish population which included statements to the effect that Plymouth was run by Jewish money-lenders and racketeers, and that the attitude of the German people to Jews, 'while regrettable was not to be wondered at' and that 'the policy and methods associated with the Jews will be among the primary objects marked for destruction before socialism will be realised' (National

177

Executive Committee 1933). It is difficult to determine whether this was an isolated incident, or how widespread such attitudes might have been in the Labour Party. Certainly the party centrally made it known that such attitudes would not be tolerated.

4 This chapter explored dominant official labour positions and indicates major areas where these are contested, especially by local party organisation. Anti-semitism is a term imposed on the discourse in order to make an analysis. It was used, though not widely at this time.

5 The British Union's predominant, though not its only contribution, to British politics was anti-semitic. Its most famous slogan 'We've got to get rid of the yids' (*New Statesman and Nation* 4 April 1936: 520) coincided with the publication in Britain of the protocols of the Learned Elders of Zion which uncovered a fake plot by Jewish financiers and communists to create a world state.

6 Corporatism in the writings of Mosley (1932) and Thompson (1947) was a theory of the state which demanded a collective approach to industrial relations and the organisation of the political community into corporate interest groups. Unlike Cole's guild socialism, which turned everyone into a producer and sustained a sovereignty of political wills, corporatism maintained the functions of producers, consumers, and above all experts, with a sovereignty invested in a single corporate leader. Corporatism contained a nationalistic and strident protectionism and propounded British superiority over other nations.

7 This has no special significance. There was British Union agitation in many other cities as well, but East London provides a good case study. It was steeped in labour traditions and organisation and provides an example of the relationship between local and central Labour Party organisation.

8 The Fascist Union of British Workers was started as a subsidiary of the British Union. Fascist newspapers like the *Fascist Week* aimed to appeal to trade unionists and, of course, caused unease in the labour movement about the extent of fascist recruitment among labour and trade union members (Labour Party 1934). It is not clear how many workers or supporters joined the British Union, or were influenced by its actions. The British Union's estimates of its own membership (featured in various *New Statesman and Nation* articles of the time) were probably inflated.

9 The Battle of Cable Street, as it was subsequently referred to, was the result of anti-fascist forces massing to prevent Mosley and his black-shirted army marching through a Jewish area of East London

in October 1936. This is the best-known street conflict between British Union supporters and anti-fascist demonstrators, though only one of many similar conflicts. It was claimed as a victory by anti-fascists, and entered labour and communist mythology as a victory against fascism.

10 It was over this point that labourist notions of fascism differed from the Communist Party. For the Communist Party, disorder (the glimmer of revolutionary upheaval) was an entirely productive force in the task of social reconstruction.

11 Statements about the barbarism of communism found in 'The Communist Solar System' (Labour Party 1933b) are references to the Soviet Union under Stalin, and formed an important part of labour's objection to communism, discussed in chapter two.

12 The Board of Deputies of Anglo Jewry was the official voice of the Jewish community in Britain. Its principal concern was Judaeism, and until 1936 it insisted that anti-semitism was not its concern. Following a concerted campaign by the *Jewish Chronicle* the board changed its mind, possibly concerned that if it did not take a stand against anti-semitism, it would be usurped as a leader of the Jewish community and opinion. It did not approve of violence or street clashes, but issued a statement of Jewish solidarity against anti-semitism and the threat of communism (Board of Deputies of Anglo Jewry 16 October 1936).

13 The issue of the extension of police powers in relation to public assembly was being discussed in the Labour Party by 1934. Labour's main concerns were to do with the militarisation of politics by the British Union, and not a need to defend the Jewish population from attack.

14 The main initiative for the United Front came from the British Communist Party. Other political forces included the Socialist League (which was formed out of the Society for Socialist Inquiry and Propaganda in 1932) and those Independent Labour Party members who, regretting disaffiliation, wanted to work with the Labour Party. The Socialist League was expelled from the Labour Party on this account in 1937 (Labour Party 1937b). The United Front was styled after the Popular Front, a French anti-fascist alliance. The question of whether labour should be involved in the United Front was a hotly contested issue in the party, raised repeatedly at conferences between 1933 and 1937. Labour bombarded its members with warnings about the consequences of participation in such an

initiative, on the grounds that it was anti-democratic and an avenue into the British labour movement for Moscow.

15 The Relief Committee for the Victims of German Fascism, which helped Austrian and German Jews at the height of nazi persecution, was a proscribed organisation, on the grounds that it was communist dominated. This provides an example of labour's blinkered approach to British politics, in which principle (in this case racial persecution) was subsidiary to organisation and strategy.

16 There were those in the Labour Party who argued that a United Front Against Fascism was unnecessary, and that fascism was not such a real possibility in Britain as in France. Opposition to fascism sustained it as a political force, and if fascist meetings were ignored it would wither (Dalton 1936: 481). This was later abandoned in favour of an official strategy which involved demonstrations and public meetings of a non- confrontational kind.

8 ANTI-RACISM IN THE 1970s

1 The National Front was formed in 1967 to give a respectable political face to a number of factions, including the League of Empire Loyalists, the British National Party, the Racial Preservation Society and the Greater Britain Movement (an off-shoot of the National Socialist Movement). The Front's prominent figures included John Tyndall and Martin Webster. The British National Party split from it in 1976, in disgust at its nazi image (Labour Party 1979: 68–9). In late 1977 the National Front was claiming a large membership and aiming at building electoral success (Taylor 1979: 130). There was concern about the size of its vote in some traditional working class areas. It faded from political prominence in the late 1970s.

2 This statement on race was taken from labour's most detailed account of race for the 1970s, used in the 1979 general election campaign (Labour Party 1979). It defends labour's record on race relations and immigration, but admits the need for changes. It suggests that racism is something built into legislation, and arising from social conditions and systems of social distribution as well as the political activities of the National Front.

3 See, for example, *Labour Weekly* 23 July 1976: 12, Somerville 9 July 1976: 12.

4 Racism, racialism and fascism are all used throughout this period to refer to the same range of political issues, though the term fascism

was more prominently used when the National Front was involved and its use faded with the decline of the National Front.

5 The concern with fascist activity of the 1930s briefly re-emerged in the late 1940s as a labour issue. In responding to fascism in the postwar period, labour repeated 1930s formulations (Finlay 1948: 179) which then lay dormant until resurrected in the late 1970s as a way of responding to the National Front.

6 Bethnal Green and Stepney Trades Council's (1978) publication *Blood on the Streets* documents some of the racial violence directed at the local Bengali population in that area of East London, and provides some striking parallels with attacks on Jews in the same area in the 1930s.

7 Not just the Labour Party, but the Communist Party, the Socialist Workers' Party, the International Marxist Group and others, all had different ideas about what the National Front stood for, and the significance of fascism and racism in British politics.

8 Racial attacks and murders were not unique to this period or confined to the Bengali, or even Asian population. Racial attacks were, and are still, recorded throughout Britain, but in the period under review they were a particularly prominent issue, because of the involvement of the National Front.

9 Although social deprivation was associated with race in the 1930s there was no attempt to deal with this aside from the 1905 Aliens Act, which restricted the entry of pauper aliens, until the 1960s and 1970s. Labour produced funding to deal with race as a dimension of social inequality through its urban funding programmes (National Executive Committee 1978: 1).

10 Labour activists were involved in the Anti-Nazi League's leadership. Four MPs joined the steering committee out of a group of forty-three who sponsored the founding statement of the movement. Benn, from the cabinet, addressed Anti-Nazi League rallies though it was not formally allied to the Labour Party, and ignored by its race policy group (Messina 1989: 119–20).

9 BLACK REPRESENTATION: PROSPECTS FOR THE 1990s

1 Bernie Grant, Diane Abbott, Paul Boateng and Keith Vaz were not the first black MPs, but the first in postwar multi-racial Britain, elected by constituencies containing substantial black populations.

2 The expulsion of Amir Khan and Kevin Scally from Sparkbrook Constituency Labour Party in 1985 was bound up with Khan's attempt to organise black sections. Scally was expelled for talking to the media about suspected black applications for party membership in his constituency party (Matharu 1986: 16).

3 Messina (1989: 141) suggests the Labour Race Action Group had been in existence since the early 1970s, and acted as a pressure group around race issues in the Labour Party. A voice criticising labour policy on immigration in the 1970s, by the 1980s it was widely supported in the constituencies and involved sixty labour MPs. Its members were on the Human Rights and Race Relations Sub-Committee by 1980, and its former chair was Keith Vaz, a prominent supporter of black sections.

4 Kingsley Abrams is the current vice chair of the Black Sections Movement, and a committed socialist produced by labour's youth wing. His past posts in the Black Sections Movement include Youth Organiser and National Secretary (Abrams 25 June 1990).

5 These are supporters and not members, so that black sections cannot be accused of being a party within a party.

6 Evidence concerning the nature of the political programme of the Black Sections Movement is only just emerging. This process will accelerate once the demand for black sections has been won, and the political energy put into this demand is diverted into the generation of a political programme to oppose racism. An important start has been made with the publication of *The Black Agenda* (Labour Party Black Section 1988).

7 Bousquet was a parliamentary candidate in the 1983 election. He has a strong labour and trade union background, involvement in black self-help organisation and in local politics. In 1983 he was Race Relations Advisor for housing in the London Borough of Lambeth. He also worked with the Black and Asian Committee.

8 The National Executive Committee's working group consisted of representatives of Labour Race Action Group, the Black Sections Movement, the Parliamentary Labour Party and Labour Party regions.

9 The minority report of the working group was signed by Rita Austin, Marion Fitzgerald and Robin Corbett MP. Black sections were sabotaged by the labour left.

10 The Black and Asian Committee's first meeting was in March 1986 and was chaired by Jo Richardson. In January 1987 it was upgraded to a full committee of the National Executive Committee.

BIBLIOGRAPHY

Abbott, D. (1987) 'Speech on Immigration', *Parliamentary Debates: Official Report* 122: 815–17.

Abbott, D. (1988) 'Speech at Annual Labour Party Conference', *The Labour Party Annual Reports*: 108–9, London: Labour Party.

Abrams, K. (25 June 1990) Author Interview, unpublished.

Adams, C. (1978) 'Speech at Annual Labour Party Conference', *The Labour Party Annual Reports*: 312–13, London: Labour Party.

Adney, M. (1970) 'Speech at Annual Labour Party Conference', *The Labour Party Annual Reports*: 206–7, London: Labour Party.

All India Congress Committee (18 July 1930) 'Report', unpublished, Nehru Memorial Library and Archives, Delhi.

—— (1929–1939) 'Records', unpublished, Nehru Memorial Library and Archives, Delhi.

Ambedkar, Dr (1930–1931) 'Speech' *Proceedings of the Round Table Conference, first session*: 131–7, London: HMSO.

Anwar, M. (1986) *Race and Politics*, London: Tavistock.

Apps, R. (1985) 'Speech at Annual Labour Party Conference', *The Labour Party Annual Reports*: 33–4, London: Labour Party.

Astbury, P. (1986) 'Speech at Annual Labour Party Conference', *The Labour Party Annual Reports*: 17–18, London: Labour Party.

Attlee, C. (1931) 'Speech on Indian Policy', *Parliamentary Debates: Official Report* 260: 1118–31.

Ball, W. and Solomos, J. (1990) *Race and Local Politics*, London: Macmillan.

Balogun, K. (1987) 'Speech at Annual Labour Party Conference', *The Labour Party Annual Reports*: 134, London: Labour Party.

Banergee, S. (10 February 1977) 'Interview Transcript', unpublished, Nehru Memorial Library and Archives, Delhi.

Banks, T. (1969) 'Speech at Annual Labour Party Conference', *The Labour Party Annual Reports*: 215–16, London: Labour Party.

Banton, M. and Harwood, J. (1975) *The Race Concept*, London: David and Charles.

Belos, L. (1986) 'Speech at Annual Labour Party Conference', *The Labour Party Annual Reports*: 60–61, London: Labour Party.

Benewick, R. (1969) *Political Violence and Public Order*, London: Allen Lane.

Benewick, R. (1972) *Fascist Movement in Britain*, London: Allen Lane.

Benn, T. (10 September 1976) 'Report of a Speech', *Labour Weekly*: 3.

Benn, T. and Heffer, E. (1986) 'A Strategy for Labour', *New Left Review* 158: 60–74.

—— (1988) 'What Now for Labour?' in E. Heffer (ed.) *Forward to Socialism*, London: Labour Party Supporters of the Benn and Heffer Campaign.

Benningfield, J. (1977) Author Interview, unpublished.

Ben-Tovim, G. and Gabriel, J. (1984) 'The Politics of Race in Britain, 1962–79: A Review of Recent Debates', in C. Husband (ed.) *Race in Britain*, London: Hutchinson.

Ben-Tovim, G., Gabriel, J., Law, I. and Stredder, K. (1986) *The Local Politics of Race*, London: Macmillan.

Bethnal Green Communist Party (undated, circa 1934–36) 'Fascism', unpublished, Bethnal Green Labour Party Collection, National Museum of Labour History, London.

Bethnal Green and Stepney Trades Council (1978) *Blood on the Streets*, London: Bethnal Green and Stepney Trades Council.

Bidwell, S. (1977) 'Speech at Annual Labour Party Conference', *The Labour Party Annual Reports*: 314, London: Labour Party.

Binns, T. (1965) 'Speech on Race Relations', *Parliamentary Debates: Official Report* 711: 1003–8.

Birmingham Centre for Contemporary Cultural Studies (1982) *The Empire Strikes Back*, London: Hutchinson.

Board of Deputies of Anglo-Jewry (16 October 1936) 'The Communist Danger', *Jewish Weekly*: 1.

Bousquet, B. (1987) 'The Reality of the Black Vote. A Discussion Paper', unpublished, Labour Party Archives.

Boyce, P. (1986) 'Speech at Annual Labour Party Conference', *The Labour Party Annual Reports*: 59–60, London: Labour Party.

Brockway, F. (1928) *Socialism with Speed*, London: ILP Publications.

—— (1931) *The I.L.P. and the Crisis*, London: ILP Publications.

—— (1932) *Socialism at the Crossroads. Why the I.L.P. Left the Labour Party*, London: ILP Publications.

—— (1961) 'Speech on Immigration', *Parliamentary Debates: Official Report* 634: 1997.

—— (1963) 'Speech on Racial Discrimination and Incitement', *Parliamentary Debates: Official Report* 670: 97–100.

—— (1977) Author Interview, unpublished.

Buchanan, Mr (1931) 'Speech on Indian Policy', *Parliamentary Debates: Official Report* 260: 1356–60.

Bullock, A. (1960) *The Life and Times of Ernest Bevin*, London: Heinemann.

Cambridge, A. X. and Feuchtwang, S. (1990) 'Histories of Racism', in A. X. Cambridge and S. Feuchtwang (eds) *Antiracist Strategies*, Aldershot: Gower.

Carless, B. (1977) 'Speech at Annual Labour Party Conference', *The Labour Party Annual Reports*: 311–12, London: Labour Party.

Charter 88 (5–6 May 1990), the *Guardian*: 15.

Charter 88 (1988) London: Charter 88.

Chater, D. (undated, circa 1936) 'Statement', unpublished, Bethnal Green Labour Party Collection, National Museum of Labour History, London.

Coates, D. (1982) 'Space and Agency in the Transition to Socialism', *New Left Review* 135: 49–61.

Cole, G.D.H. (1931) *For Those Over 21 Only*, London: Society for Socialist Inquiry and Propaganda.

—— (1961) *History of Socialist Thought* 4, 1, London: Macmillan.

—— (1969) *A History of the Labour Party from 1914*, London: Routledge and Kegan Paul.

Cope, F. (1977) 'Speech at Annual Labour Party Conference', *The Labour Party Annual Reports*: 309–310, London: Labour Party.

Cousins, M. and Hussain, A. (1984) *Michel Foucault*, London: Macmillan.

Cripps, S. (1932) 'Speech at Annual Labour Party Conference', *The Labour Party Annual Reports*: 286, London: Labour Party.

—— (1933) 'Speech at Annual Labour Party Conference', *The Labour Party Annual Reports*: 159–60, London: Labour Party.

Cutler, A., Hindess, B., Hirst, P. and Hussain, A. (1977) *Marx's Capital and Capitalism Today*, 1, London: Routledge and Kegan Paul.

Daily Herald (1 October 1936) 'Lansbury Advises People to Keep Away from Fascist Demonstration': 1.

Daily Herald (5 October 1936) 'Street Battle Stops Mosley March': 1.

Daily Herald (15 October 1936) 'Headline': 1.

Dalton, H. (1936) 'The Popular Front', *Political Quarterly* 7: 481–9.

Davies, R. (May 1933) 'Letter to the Labour Party', unpublished, National Executive Committee Records, Labour Party Archives.

Davis, C. (1972) 'Speech on Commonwealth Immigrants', *Parliamentary Debates: Official Report* 842: 868.

Driberg, T. (1967) 'Speech at Annual Labour Party Conference', *The Labour Party Annual Reports*: 316–17, London: Labour Party.

—— (1970) 'Speech at Annual Labour Party Conference', *The Labour Party Annual Reports*: 208–9, London: Labour Party.

Duff-Cooper, A. (15 October 1936) 'Making City Hideous', *Daily Herald*: 2.

Dukes, C. E. (1934) 'Speech at Annual Labour Party Conference', *The Labour Party Annual Reports*: 142–3, London: Labour Party.

Durbin, E. (1935) 'Democracy and Socialism in Britain', *Political Quarterly* 6: 379–85.

—— (1940) *The Politics of Democratic Socialism*, London: Routledge and Kegan Paul.

Ennals, J. (1976) 'Speech at Annual Labour Party Conference', *The Labour Party Annual Reports*: 220–1, London: Labour Party.

Feuchtwang, S. (1980) 'Socialist, Feminist and Anti- Racist Struggles', *mf* 4: 41–55.

—— (1982) 'Occupational Ghettoes', *Economy and Society* 11, 3: 251–91.

Finlay, B. (1948) 'Speech at Annual Labour Party Conference', *The Annual Reports of the Labour Party*: 179–80, London: Labour Party.

185

Fishman, W. J. (1975) *East End Jewish Radicals*, London: Duckworth.

Floud, B. (1965) 'Speech on the Race Relations Bill', *Parliamentary Debates: Official Report* 711: 970–1.

Foot, P. (1965) *Immigration and Race in British Politics*, Harmondsworth: Penguin.

Foucault, M. (1972) *The Archaeology of Knowledge*, New York: Pantheon Books.

Furnival, J. S. (1939) *Netherlands India*, Cambridge: Cambridge University Press.

Garland, R. (1977) 'Speech at Annual Labour Party Conference', *The Labour Party Annual Reports*: 308–9, London: Labour Party.

Garrard, J. A. (1971) *The English and Immigration 1880–1910*, London: OUP.

Gartner, L. P. (1973) *The Jewish Immigrant in England 1870–1914*, London: Simon Publications.

Gidney, Lt. Col. (1930–1931) 'Speech', *Proceedings of the Round Table Conference First Session*: 72–6.

Gilroy, P. (1987) *There Ain't No Black in the Union Jack*, London: Tavistock.

Goodman, P. (1988) 'Speech at Annual Labour Party Conference', *The Labour Party Annual Reports*: 106, London: Labour Party.

Gordon, M. (1982) 'Speech at Annual Labour Party Conference', *The Labour Party Annual Reports*: 11–12, London: Labour Party.

Grant, T. (1989) *The Unbroken Thread. The Development of Trotskyism Over 40 Years*, London: Fortress Books.

Haldane Club (1935) 'Report on the Desirability of Legislation Against Political Uniforms with Drafts of Such Legislation', unpublished, Records of the New Fabian Research Bureau, Nuffield College Oxford.

Hattersley, R. (1982) 'Speech at Annual Labour Party Conference', *The Labour Party Annual Reports*: 226–7, London: Labour Party.

—— (1985) 'Speech at Annual Labour Party Conference', *The Labour Party Annual Reports*: 37–9, London: Labour Party.

Hawkins, A. (1977) 'Speech at Annual Labour Party Conference', *The Labour Party Annual Reports*: 310–11, London: Labour Party.

Heath, F. J. (1934) 'Speech at Annual Labour Party Conference', *The Labour Party Annual Reports*: 135–6, London: Labour Party.

Henderson, A. (1961) 'Speech on Control of Immigration', *Parliamentary Debates: Official Report* 634: 1958–62.

Hendon South Constituency Labour Party (5 May 1977) 'Minutes', unpublished, Archives at Hendon Library.

—— (12 August 1977) 'Minutes', unpublished, Archives at Hendon Library.

—— (14 December 1977) 'Minutes', unpublished, Archives at Hendon Library.

—— (1983) 'Resolution on Positive Discrimination Moved at Annual Labour Party Conference', *The Labour Party Annual Reports*: 260.

Hoare, Q. and Ali, T. (1982) 'Socialists and the Crisis of Labourism', *New Left Review* 132: 59–81.

Hobbes, T. (1970) *Leviathan*, London: Dent and Sons.

Hoey, C. (1978) 'Speech at Annual Labour Party Conference', *The Labour Party Annual Reports*: 316–17, London: Labour Party.

Home Affairs Department (1930) *Indian Statutory Commission Report 1,* London: HMSO.
—— (1936) *Public Order Act,* London: HMSO.
Home Office (1965a) *Race Relations Act,* London: HMSO.
—— (1965b) *Immigration from the Commonwealth,* London: HMSO.
—— (1968a) *Commonwealth Immigration Act,* London: HMSO.
—— (1968b) *Race Relations Act,* London: HMSO.
—— (1971) *Immigration Act,* London: HMSO.
—— (1976) *Race Relations Act,* London: HMSO.
—— (1978) 'Letter to the Anti-Racist Committee of Bethnal Green and Stepney Trades Council', in *Blood on the Streets,* London: Bethnal Green and Stepney Trades Council.
—— (1981) *British Nationality Act,* London: HMSO.
—— (1988) *Immigration Act,* London: HMSO.
Howe, S. and Upshall, D. (15 July 1988) 'New Black Power Lines', *New Statesman and Society* 1, 6: 12–13.
Husband, C. (1984) 'Introduction: "Race." The Continuity of a Concept', in C. Husband (ed.) *Race in Britain,* London: Hutchinson.
Hutchinson, H. L. (1936) 'Speech at Annual Labour Party Conference', *The Labour Party Annual Reports*: 221, London: Labour Party.
Hyacinth, F. (1987) 'Speech at Annual Labour Party Conference', *The Labour Party Annual Reports*: 135, London: Labour Party.
Hynd, H. (1961) 'Speech on Control of Immigration', *Parliamentary Debates: Official Report* 634: 1937.
India Office (1930–1931) *Proceedings of the Round Table Conference First Session,* London: HMSO.
—— (1931a) *Proceedings of the Round Table Conference Second Session,* London: HMSO.
—— (1931b) *Royal Commission on Labour in India Report,* London: HMSO.
Inskip, Sir P. (15 October 1936) 'Few Misguided People', *Daily Herald*: 2.
Jenkins, R. (1966) 'Speech at National Co-ordinating Conference of Voluntary Liaison Committees for Commonwealth Immigrants', in Labour Party (1967) 'Immigration and Race Relations', *Information Paper*, 22, London: Labour Party.
—— (1973) 'Speech on Immigration and Race Relations', *Parliamentary Debates: Official Report* 865: 1485–98.
—— (1976) 'Speech on Immigration and Emigration', *Parliamentary Debates: Official Report* 912: 94–104.
—— (30 July 1976) 'Speech' reported in 'The Way to Hit Back at Racialism', *Labour Weekly*: 7.
Jewish Chronicle (9 September 1938) *'Jewish Defence'*: 21.
—— (9 December 1938) 'Jewish Defence': 2.
Johnson, D. (1988) 'Speech at Annual Labour Party Conference', *The Labour Party Annual Reports*: 107, London: Labour Party.
Johnson, J. (1969) 'Speech at Annual Labour Party Conference', The Labour Party Annual Reports: 218, London: Labour Party.
Johnson, W. H. (1965) 'Speech at Annual Labour Party Conference', *The Labour Party Annual Reports*: 215–17, London: Labour Party.

Joint Consultative Committee of the London Trades Council and the London Labour Party (1934) 'The Labour Movement and Fascism: A Special Memorandum', *Circular*, London: Labour Party.

Jones, G. S. (1976) *Outcast London*, Harmondsworth: Penguin.

Jones, M. (1931) 'Speech on Indian Policy', *Parliamentary Debates: Official Report* 260: 1326–36.

Kelly, J. (1985) 'Speech at Annual Labour Party Conference', *The Labour Party Annual Reports*: 276–7, London: Labour Party.

Kinnock, N. (1987) 'Statement on Race Equality', unpublished, Labour Party Archives.

Knights, R. (1977) 'Speech at Annual Labour Party Conference', *The Labour Party Annual Reports*: 313, London: Labour Party.

Knowles, C. (1979) 'Labour and Anti-Semitism: An account of the political discourse surrounding the Labour Party's involvement with anti-semitism in East London, 1934–6', in R. Miles and A. Phizacklea (eds) *Racism and Political Action in Britain*, London: Routledge and Kegan Paul.

Knowles, C. and Mercer, S. (1990) 'Feminism and Anti-Racism: An Exploration of the Political Possibilities', in A. X. Cambridge and S. Feuchtwang (eds) *Antiracist Strategies*, Aldershot: Gower.

Kuper, L. and Smith, M. G. (1971) *Pluralism in Africa*, Los Angeles: African Studies Center.

Labour Party (1928) 'Labour and the Nation', in New Fabian Research Bureau Records (1932), Nuffield College Oxford.

—— (1929) 'Constitution and Standing Orders', *The Labour Party Annual Reports*: 2–10, London: Labour Party.

—— (1930a) 'Report on the League Against Imperialism', *The Labour Party Annual Reports*: 33–4, London: Labour Party.

—— (1930b) 'Statement on Palestine', *Policy Statement*, London: Labour Party.

—— (1933a) 'Socialism and the Condition of the People', Policy Statement, London: Labour Party.

—— (1933b) 'The Communist Solar System', *Policy Statement*, London: Labour Party.

—— (1933c) 'The Colonies', *Policy Statement*, London: Labour Party.

—— (1934) 'Fascism at Home and Abroad', *Policy Statement*, London: Labour Party.

—— (undated, circa 1937a) 'The British Labour Movement and Communism', *Policy Statement*, London: Labour Party.

—— (1937b) 'Labour and the So Called Unity Campaign', *Policy Statement*, London: Labour Party.

—— (1937c) 'Party Loyalty: An Appeal to the Movement', *Circular*, London: Labour Party.

—— (1957) 'Final Draft Statement on Racial Prejudice', unpublished, Labour Party Archives.

—— (1958) 'Racial Discrimination', *Policy Statement*, London: Labour Party.

—— (1959) 'Britain Belongs to You', Election Manifesto, in *The Labour Party Annual Reports*, appendix, London: Labour Party.

188

—— (1962) 'Statement on Racial Hatred', *The Labour Party Annual Reports*: 197, London: Labour Party.

—— (1964) 'The Labour Party and Commonwealth Immigration', *Policy Statement*, London: Labour Party.

—— (1967a) *Report of the Race Relations Working Party*, London: Labour Party.

—— (1967b) 'Racial Discrimination', *Policy Statement*, London: Labour Party.

—— (1968a) 'Immigration Restrictions', *Information Paper* 22, London: Labour Party.

—— (1968b) 'The Tory Stand on Immigration', *Talking Points Pamphlet* 21, London: Labour Party.

—— (1972a) 'Citizenship, Immigration and Integration', *Policy Statement*, London: Labour Party.

—— (1972b) 'Report from the Home Policy Committee', unpublished, National Executive Committee Records.

—— (1976) 'Parliamentary Report', *The Labour Party Annual Reports*: 100–101, London: Labour Party.

—— (1977) 'Statement on Race', *The Labour Party Annual Reports*: 308, London: Labour Party.

—— (1979) *Campaign Handbook. Race, Immigration and the Racialists*, London: Labour Party.

—— (1980a) 'British Nationality Law', *Policy Statement*, London: Labour Party.

—— (1980b) 'The Tories' Immigration Proposals', *Information Paper*, London: Labour Party.

—— (1980c) 'Labour and the Black Electorate', *Advice Note 1*, London: Labour Party.

—— (1980d) 'Questionnaire' unpublished, National Executive Committee Records.

—— (1981a) 'Race, Immigration and Nationality – the Tory Record May 1979–March 1981', *Information Paper 20*, London: Labour Party.

—— (1981b) 'British Nationality Law – Our Alternative to Tory Legislation', *Policy Statement*, London: Labour Party.

—— (1982) *Labour's Programme*, London: Labour Party.

—— (1983a) 'Race, Nationality and Immigration – the Tory Record', *Information Paper 50*, London: Labour Party.

—— (1983b) 'Talking Points', *Pamphlet*, London: Labour Party.

—— (1985a) 'Constitution and Standing Orders', *The Labour Party Annual Reports*: 287–97, London: Labour Party.

—— (1985b) *Positive Discrimination/Black People and the Labour Party*, London: Labour Party.

—— (1986a) 'Black People and the Labour Party', *Newsletter*, London: Labour Party.

—— (1986b) 'Annual Labour Party Conference Debate on Disciplinary Procedures', *The Labour Party Annual Reports*: 13–19, London: Labour Party.

—— (1987) 'Ethnic Minorities', *Background Briefing* 21, London: Labour Party.

189

—— (1988) 'Social Justice and Economic Efficiency', *First Report of Labour's Policy Review for the 1990s*, London: Labour Party.

—— (1989) 'Meet the Challenge, Make the Change. A New Agenda for Britain', *Final Report of Labour's Policy Review for the 1990s*, London: Labour Party.

—— (July 1989) 'Multi-Cultural Education. Labour's Policy for Schools', *Policy Statement*, London: Labour Party.

—— (September 1989) 'Race Equality', *Newsletter 1*, London: Labour Party.

Labour Party Black Section (1988) *The Black Agenda*, London: Labour Party Black Section.

Labour Weekly (4 February 1972) 'Women to Help Immigrants': 10.

Labour Weekly (23 July 1976) 'Letters Commenting on Racism in the Labour Party': 12.

Labour Weekly (30 July 1976) 'National Affront': 5.

Labour Weekly (20 August 1976) 'Front for Tories': 5.

Lansbury, G. (1931) 'Speech on Indian Policy', *Parliamentary Debates: Official Report* 260: 1390–9.

—— (1929–1935) 'Personal Papers', unpublished, Passfield Collection, British Library of Political and Economic Science.

—— (1935) *Jesus and Labour*, London: ILP Publications.

Larkin, J. (1967) 'Speech at Annual Labour Party Conference', *The Labour Party Annual Reports*: 313–14, London: Labour Party.

Leopold, J. (1974) 'The British Application of Aryan Race Theory to India 1850–70', *English Historical Review* 89, 352: 578–603.

Lerner, G. (1976) 'Speech at Annual Labour Party Conference', *The Labour Party Annual Reports*: 213–15, London: Labour Party.

Lester, A. and Bindman, G. (1972) *Race and Law*, Harmondsworth: Penguin.

Lestor, J. (1972) 'Speech at Annual Labour Party Conference', *The Labour Party Annual Reports*: 157–8, London: Labour Party.

—— (1976) 'Speech on Immigration and Emigration', *Parliamentary Debates: Official Report* 912: 73–9.

Lestor, J. (15 October 1976) 'Now is the Time to Hit Back at Racism', *Labour Weekly*: 6.

—— (1982) 'Speech at Annual Labour Party Conference', *The Labour Party Annual Reports*: 227–8, London: Labour Party.

Levenberg, Dr (1977) Author Interview, unpublished.

Locke, J. (1970) *Two Treatises on Civil Government*, London: Dent and Sons.

Lyon, A. (1976a) 'Speech on Immigration and Emigration', *Parliamentary Debates: Official Report* 912: 55–68.

—— (1976b) 'Speech at Annual Labour Party Conference', *The Labour Party Annual Reports*: 221–5, London: Labour Party.

MacDonald, R. (1931) 'Speech on Indian Policy', *Parliamentary Debates: Official Report* 260: 1101–8.

Maine, H. (1965) *Ancient Law*, London: Dent and Sons.

Marwa, S. S. (1984) 'Speech at Annual Labour Party Conference', *The Labour Party Annual Reports*: 169–70, London: Labour Party.

Matharu, J. (1986) 'Speech at Annual Labour Party Conference', *The Labour Party Annual Reports*: 16–17, London: Labour Party.

Merrell, J. (1985) 'Speech at Annual Labour Party Conference', *The Labour Party Annual Reports*: 227–8, London: Labour Party.

Mesbahuddin, A. (1987) *The British Labour Party and the Indian Independence Movement 1917–39*, London: Oriental University Press.

Messina, A. M. (1989) *Race and Party Competition in Britain*, London: Clarendon Press.

Miles, R. (1982) *Racism and Migrant Labour*, London: Routledge and Kegan Paul.

—— (1989) *Racism*, London: Routledge.

Miles, R. and Phizacklea, A. (1979a) 'Working Class Racist Beliefs in the Inner City', in R. Miles and A. Phizacklea (eds) *Racism and Political Action in Britain*, London: Routledge and Kegan Paul.

—— (1979b) 'Some Introductory Observations on Race and Politics in Britain', in R. Miles and A. Phizacklea (eds) *Racism and Political Action in Britain*, London: Routledge and Kegan Paul.

—— (1980) *Labour and Racism*, London: Routledge and Kegan Paul.

Miliband, R. (1975) *Parliamentary Socialism. A Study in the Politics of Labour*, London: Merlin Press.

Mill, J. S. (1968) *Utilitarianism, Liberty and Representative Government*, London: Dent and Sons.

Mody, Mr (1930) 'Speech', *Proceedings of the Round Table Conference First Session*: 155–7, London: HMSO.

Montesquieu, C. S. (1949) *The Spirit of the Laws*, London: Hatner.

Moore, R. (1975) *Racism and Black Resistance in Britain*, London: Pluto Press.

Moore, R. and Wallace, T. (1975) *Slamming the Door*, London: Martin Robertson.

Morrison, H. (1933) 'Speech at Annual Labour Party Conference', *The Labour Party Annual Reports*: 219, London: Labour Party.

Morrison, H. (1936) 'Speech at Annual Labour Party Conference', *The Labour Party Annual Reports*: 114–16, London: Labour Party.

Mosley, O. (1932) *Great Britain*, London: BUF Publications.

Movement for Colonial Freedom (1960) *Annual Report*, London: Movement for Colonial Freedom.

Murray, L. and Keys, B. (1978) 'Statement on Race Relations in East London' in Bethnal Green and Stepney Trades Council, *Blood on the Streets*, London: Bethnal Green and Stepney Trades Council.

National Council for Civil Liberties (1936) 'Letter to the Mayor of Bethnal Green', unpublished, Bethnal Green Labour Party Collection, National Museum of Labour History, London.

National Executive Committee of the Labour Party (1930) 'Draft Resolutions on Indian Political Prisoners', unpublished NEC Records, Labour Party Archives.

—— (1933) 'Minutes', unpublished NEC Records, Labour Party Archives.

—— (1978) 'Response to the National Front', *Policy Statement*, London: Labour Party.

191

—— (1982) 'Immigration: Labour's Approach', *Statement to Annual Labour Party Conference*, London: Labour Party.

—— (1985) 'Statement on Events in Brixton', *Press Release*, London: Labour Party.

National Joint Council of the Labour Party (1933a) 'Meerut Release the Prisoners', *Policy Statement*, London: Labour Party.

—— (1933b) 'Democracy Versus Dictatorship', *Policy Statement*, London: Labour Party.

—— (1934a) 'Minutes', unpublished NJC Records, Labour Party Archives.

—— (1934b) 'Resolution on Fascism', unpublished NJC Records, Labour Party Archives.

—— (1934c) 'Statement to the Movement', *Circular*, London: Labour Party.

—— (1934d) 'Fascism at Home and Abroad', *The Labour Party Annual Reports*: 294–308, London: Labour Party.

New Fabian Research Bureau (1928) 'Collection of Labour Party Statements on India', unpublished, Records of the New Fabian Research Bureau, Nuffield College Oxford.

New Fabian Research Bureau (1931) 'Letter to the Labour Party on the Foundation of the Bureau', unpublished, Records of the New Fabian Research Bureau, Nuffield College Oxford.

New Statesman and Nation (16 June 1934) 'The Black Army': 904–5.

—— (3 November 1934) 'A London Diary': 615–16.

—— (4 April 1936) 'Editorial': 520.

—— (10 October 1936) 'Fascism and the Jews': 496–7.

North East Bethnal Green Council (May 1936) 'Minutes', unpublished, Bethnal Green Labour Party Collection, National Museum of Labour History, London.

North East Bethnal Green Labour Party (1934) 'Circular', Bethnal Green Labour Party Collection, National Museum of Labour History, London.

Nugent, N. and King, R. (1979) 'Ethnic Minorities, Scapegoating and the Extreme Right', in R. Miles and A. Phizacklea (eds) *Racism and Political Action in Britain*, London: Routledge and Kegan Paul.

Ouseley, H. (1990) 'Resisting Institutional Change', in W. Ball and J. Solomos (eds) *Race and Local Politics*, London: Macmillan.

Padover, S. (1943) *The Complete Jefferson*, New York: Duell Sloane and Pearce.

Parkin, B. T. (1961) 'Speech on Immigration', *Parliamentary Debates: Official Report* 634: 1942–51.

Parliamentary Debates: Official Report (1961) 'Debate on Control of Immigration' 634: 1929–2024.

Patil, M. (1988) 'Speech at Annual Labour Party Conference', *The Labour Party Annual Reports*: 106–7, London: Labour Party.

Pimlott, B. (1977) *Labour and the Left in the 1930s*, Cambridge: Cambridge University Press.

Poale Zion (1935) 'Statement Supporting the Labour Party', *Labour Party Archives*, London: Poale Zion.

—— (1936) 'Resolution on Fascism and Anti-Semitism', unpublished, Bethnal Green Labour Party Collection, National Museum of Labour History, London.

Profitt, R. (1985) 'Speech at Annual Labour Party Conference', *The Labour Party Annual Reports*: 30–1, London: Labour Party.

Rees, M. (1976) 'Speech at Annual Labour Party Conference', *The Labour Party Annual Reports*: 218–19, London: Labour Party.

—— (19 November 1976) 'The Facts of Racialism', *Labour Weekly*: 5.

—— (1977) 'Statement to Annual Labour Party Conference as Home Secretary', *The Labour Party Annual Reports*: 312–13, London: Labour Party.

Rex, J. (1986) *Race and Ethnicity*, Milton Keynes: Open University Press.

Rex, J. and Tomlinson, S. (1979) *Colonial Migrants in a British City*, London: Routledge and Kegan Paul.

Roberts, H. (7 November 1936) 'Jew and Blackshirt in the East End', *New Statesman and Nation*: 698–9.

Rose, H. (1973) 'The Politics of Immigration After the 1971 Act', *Political Quarterly* 44: 183–96.

Rousseau, J.-J. (1973) *The Social Contract and Discourses*, London: Dent and Sons.

Royle, C. (1961) 'Speech on Control of Immigration', *Parliamentary Debates: Official Report* 634: 1969–78.

Rustin, M. (1989) 'A Constitution for a Pluralist Democracy?', in P. Alcock, A. Gamble, I. Gough, P. Lee, and A. Walker (eds) *The Social Economy of the Democratic State*, London: Lawrence and Wishart.

Sapper, A. (1986) 'Speech at Annual Labour Party Conference', *The Labour Party Annual Reports*: 60, London: Labour Party.

Scarman, Lord (1981) *The Brixton Disorders 10–12 April, 1981: a report of an inquiry*, London: HMSO.

Sharma, V. (20 July 1988) Author Interview, unpublished.

—— (20 June 1990) Author Interview, unpublished.

Simon, J. (1936) 'Parliamentary Answers', *Parliamentary Debates: Official Report* 313: 1158.

Skidelsky, R. (1975) *Oswald Mosley*, London: Macmillan.

Smith, E. C. (1948) 'Speech at Annual Labour Party Conference', *The Labour Party Annual Reports*: 81, London: Labour Party.

Society for Socialist Inquiry and Propaganda (1932) 'Draft Report', unpublished, Records of the Society for Socialist Inquiry and Propaganda, Nuffield College Oxford.

Solomos, J. (1989) *Race and Racism in Contemporary Britain*, London: Macmillan.

Solomos, J. and Singh, G. (1990) 'Racial Equality, Housing and the Local State', in W. Ball, and J. Solomos (eds) *Race and Local Politics*, London: Macmillan.

Somerville, D. (9 July 1976) 'Letter', *Labour Weekly*: 12.

Soskice, F. (1965a) 'Speech on the Race Relations Bill', *Parliamentary Debates: Official Report* 716: 970–3.

—— (1965b) 'Speech on the Second Reading of the Race Relations Bill', *Parliamentary Debates: Official Report* 711: 926–39.

Sourani, M. (1986) 'Speech at Annual Labour Party Conference', *The Labour Party Annual Reports*: 61, London: Labour Party.

Sparkbrook Constituency Labour Party (1982) 'Resolution to Annual Labour Party Conference', *The Labour Party Annual Reports*: 224–5.

Springhall Communist Party (1 October 1936) 'Telegram to the Mayor of Bethnal Green', unpublished, Bethnal Green Labour Party Collection, National Museum of Labour History, London.

Stocking, G. (1969) *Race, Culture and Evolution*, London: Collier Macmillan.

Straw, J. (1983) 'Speech at Annual Labour Party Conference', *The Labour Party Annual Reports*: 73–4, London: Labour Party.

Summerskill, S. (1972) 'Speech on Illegal Immigration and Employment', *Parliamentary Debates: Official Report* 933: 1995–2000.

Taylor, S. (1976) 'Speech at Annual Labour Party Conference', *The Labour Party Annual Reports*: 216–17, London: Labour Party.

Taylor, Stan (1979) 'The National Front: Anatomy of a Political Movement', in R. Miles and A. Phizacklea (eds) *Racism and Political Action in Britain*, London: Routledge and Kegan Paul.

Tempia, M. (1981) 'Speech at Annual Labour Party Conference', *The Labour Party Annual Reports*: 253–4, London: Labour Party.

The Times (19 June 1931) 'Hindu–Mohamedan Relations': 10.

The Times of India (13 January 1931) 'Canadian Model for India': 1.

Thompson, A. R. (1947) *The Coming Corporate State*, London: Raven Books.

Trades Union Congress (1934) 'Conference Resolution', unpublished, NJC Records, Labour Party Archives.

Trades Union Congress and the Labour Party (undated, circa 1978) 'The National Front is a Nazi Front', *Pamphlet*, London: Labour Party.

Trades Union Federation (1929) 'Constitution', unpublished, Trades Union Federation Records, Nehru Memorial Library and Archives, Delhi.

—— (1929–1932) 'Minutes and Other Records', unpublished, Trades Union Federation Records, Nehru Memorial Library and Archives, Delhi.

Trades Union Federation (1933–1935) 'Records', unpublished Nehru Memorial Library and Archives, Delhi.

United Kingdom Immigrants' Advisory Service (1988) *Annual Report*, London: United Kingdom Immigrants' Advisory Service.

Wainwright, H. (1987) 'The Limits of Labourism: 1987 and Beyond', *New Left Review* 164: 34–50.

Wedgwood, Colonel (1931) 'Speech on Indian Policy', *Parliamentary Debates: Official Report* 260: 1145–54.

Whine, N. (1948) 'Speech at Annual Labour Party Conference', *The Labour Party Annual Reports*: 181, London: Labour Party.

Whitehead, P. (1976) 'Speech on Immigration', *Parliamentary Debates: Official Report* 914: 1023–30.

Williams, S. (1973) 'Speech on Illegal Immigrants', *Parliamentary Debates: Official Report* 858: 1405–13.

Wilson, H. (1968) 'Oral Answers on Racial Integration', *Parliamentary Debates: Official Report* 761: 1155–7.

Winnick, D. (1967) 'Speech at Annual Labour Party Conference', *The Labour Party Annual Report*: 315–16, London: Labour Party.

Wise, Mr (1931) 'Speech on Indian Policy', *Parliamentary Debates: Official Report* 260: 1360–3.

Woolf, L. S. (1933) *Imperialism and Civilization*, London: Hogarth Press.

—— (1933) 'Labour's Foreign Policy', *Political Quarterly* 4: 504–17.

—— (1947) *Foreign Policy. The Labour Party's Dilemma*, London: Fabian Publications.

—— (1967) *Downhill all the Way: An Autobiography of the Years 1919–1939*, Volume 4, London: Hogarth Press.

NAME INDEX

Rees, M. 104, 136, 137, 138
Rex, J. 12, 13
Richardson, J. 182
Roberts, H. 68, 69–71
Rose, H. 176
Rousseau, J.-J. 164
Royle, C. 94, 99
Russell, B. 167
Rustin, M. 38, 146

Sapper, A. 153
Saville, J. 18
Scally, K. 182
Sharma, V. 150, 152, 159
Simon, J. 116
Singh, G. 148
Sivanandan, A. 14
Skidelsky, R. 110, 172
Smith, E.C. 132
Smith, M.G. 164
Society for Socialist Inquiry and
    Propaganda 167
Solomos, J.: (1989) 24, 71, 76,
    126, 166, 175; Ball and (1990)
    166; and Singh (1990) 148
Somerville, D. 180
Soskice, F. 79, 84–7, 174
Sourani, M. 157
Sparkbrook Constituency
    Labour Party 151
Springhall Communist Party 119
Stocking, G. 63, 165
Straw, J. 42
Summerskill, S. 176

Taylor, S. 83
Taylor, Stan 127, 180
Tempia, M. 146, 147
Thatcher, M. 26, 35
Thompson, A.R. 178
Times, The 49
Times of India, The 58
Tomlinson, S. 12, 13
Trades Union Congress 114
Trades Union Congress and the
    Labour Party 131, 132
Trades Union Federation 57, 171
Tylor, E.B. 63
Tyndall, J. 180

UK Immigrants' Advisory
    Service 104
Upshall, D. 147, 156

Vaz, K. 149, 152, 156, 181, 182

Wainwright, H. 21
Wallace, T. 23, 103
Webb, B. and S. 30
Weber, M. 13
Webster, M. 180
Wedgwood, Colonel 48, 58
Whine, N. 180
Whitehead, P. 79
Williams, S. 176
Wilson, H. 77, 102
Winnick, D. 77, 86
Wise, Mr 48, 60
Woolf, L.S. 30, 167

SUBJECT INDEX

Africa 77
alien status 66
Aliens Act (1905) 71, 94
All India Socialist Party 47
All India Trades Union Congress 57
Anglo-Indians 45, 54, 55, 56, 60
Anti-Nazi League 133, 139
anti-racism: constraints in 1930s 110–12; fascism in 1930s 112–17, 121–3; fascism in 1970s 132; in 1930s 109–10; in 1970s 125; labour response to anti-semitism 5; labour strategy in 1930s 117–21; labour strategy in 1970s 138–40; local labour parties 24, 119, 133
anti-semitism 66–75; attacks on Jews 17, 72, 111, 112–13, 119; British Union of Fascists 110–12; class politics 5, 15; defence of Jews 5, *see also* Jewish defence; labour's response 3, 5, 23; National Front 131; racism 17, *see also* racism
Aryans 64
Asians: East African 102; racial attacks on 17, 81; voters 144
assimilation 74, 102
Association of Jewish Ex-Servicemen 116

Bangladeshi community 136
Battle of Cable Street *see* Cable Street
Bengali population 134
Bethnal Green 68, 119, 133, 134
betrayal thesis 23, 24
Biafra 77
Birmingham: 1970s disturbances 126; Sparkbrook Constituency Labour Party 150
black (term) 80
Black Agenda 40, 153, 154–5
Black and Asian Committee 152, 156–61
black Britons: defence of 124, 134–5, 136; labour's perceptions 140–1
black commonwealth citizenship 58–9
black councillors 148
black labour constituency 87–8
Black Liberator 76
black MPs 2, 149, 152–3, 156, 162
black representation 142–3
black rights 40–1
black sections 151–6; constituency labour parties 2; debates 138; demand for 5
Black Sections Annual Conference 153
Black Sections Movement, Labour Party 40
Black Shirts 81, 112, 119
'black solidarity day' 140
Black Trade Union Solidarity Group 152

200